The Complete
INDIAN WINE GUIDE

Dr Aakash Singh Rathore studied Enology in both the USA and Europe, and is a Certified Wine Advisor. He has written several articles on wine in Indian and international papers, and serves as a wine consultant both in India and abroad. He also studied Philosophy and Law in the USA, Brussels, Budapest, and Berlin, and is currently a Reader in the Department of Philosophy at the University of Delhi.

The Complete
INDIAN WINE GUIDE

An Illustrated
Companion to All
Domestic Indian Wines
and All Major
International Wines in
the Indian Market

Dr Aakash
Singh Rathore

LOTUS COLLECTION
ROLI BOOKS

CONTENTS

ACKNOWLEDGEMENTS   7

PREFACE   8

INTRODUCTION: 11
The Chequered History, Booming Present,
and Promising Future of Indian Wine

PART I: 17
WINE BASICS—WHAT WINE IS
AND HOW TO APPRECIATE IT

   ✣ The Three Steps of Wine Tasting
   ✣ Wine and Health
   ✣ What Wine Is
   ✣ Wine Etiquette—Moving Beyond the Myths
   ✣ Pairing Food and Wine
   ✣ Storage of Wine
   ✣ Serving Wine

PART II: 37
COMPLETE GUIDE TO ALL
DOMESTIC INDIAN WINES

   ✣ Bluefolds (Blue Star Agro Winery)
   ✣ Bosca (Baramati Grape Industries)
   ✣ Dajeebah Wines (Datacone Wine Industry)
   ✣ Flamingo Wines
   ✣ Greno Vineyards (Greengold Wines)
   ✣ Grover Vineyards
   ✣ Indage (Champagne Indage)
   ✣ N.C. Fine Wines (Fouray)
   ✣ N.D. Wines
   ✣ Prathamesh Wines
   ✣ Princess (In-Vogue Creations)
   ✣ Pyramid Wines
   ✣ Rajdheer Wines
   ✣ Saikripa Winery (Saee Group)
   ✣ Sailo Wines (V.M. Agrosoft)

- ✤ Shaw Wallace
- ✤ Sula Vineyards (Samant Soma Wines)
- ✤ Vinbros & Co
- ✤ Vinicola
- ✤ Vinsura (Sankalp Winery)
- ✤ Other Wineries Currently
  Being Developed

PART III: 99
INTERNATIONAL WINES:
COMPLETE GUIDE FOR INDIA

- ✦ Wines of the World—An Overview

- ✦ World Wines Widely Available in India
  - ✤ Imported Wines Bottled and Labelled by
    India's Domestic Producers
  - ✤ Indage Joint Ventures
  - ✤ Sula's Bottled-in-India Wines
  - ✤ Shaw Wallace's *Papillon*
  - ✤ International Bottled-in-Origin Wines
    Distributed by Domestic Producers
  - ✤ Sula Selections
  - ✤ Shaw Wallace Wines

- ✦ World Wines Imported by the International Firms
  - ✤ Henkell   ✤ Georges Duboeuf
  - ✤ Barton & Guestier ✤ E. & J. Gallo

APPENDICES: 163
  - **I:** The Best Wines and
        Best Wine Buys in India
  - **II:** Glossary & Pronunciation Guide

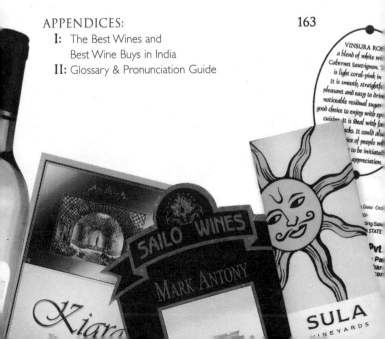

ACKNOWLEDGEMENTS

When I began research for this book there were only one or two companies in India producing a beverage that could conscionably be called 'wine'. I envisaged my task as basically creating a pamphlet or brochure on 'Wine in India and Indian Wine'—a project that would take me, at most, one month to complete. Now there are a dozen major wine producers in the country, and over 250 types of international wines available in Delhi restaurants alone. What I thought would take me a month has taken nearly two years!

But what has taken me nearly two years would have easily taken me more than 20 were it not for the help of numerous people, only a fraction of whom I can list here.

I would like to express my gratitude to Subash Arora, President of the Delhi Wine Club, for discussing the Indian wine scene with me. Balajirao B.K., President of the Hyderabad Wine Club, has also been helpful throughout. Venki, pioneer of the Indian Wine web page (*www.indianwine.com*) has been a valuable source of information. Vikram Achanta, CEO of Tulleeho (*www.tulleeho.com*), also deserves special mention. Tulleeho's website is certainly an important focal point of the Indian wine scene.

Among the producers, I am indebted to all the wineries covered in this book for permitting me to reproduce labels, and for showing me the works. Nevertheless, I must point out that I have never allowed my interaction with any of the domestic or international wine producers covered in this work to alter my objective evaluation of the quality and value of their products.

Finally, I cannot forget to mention the constant support of my family in the US and India, of my wife, Dr Devyani Khobragade, and her family. They are collectively the *sine qua non* of the appearance of this book.

Any book of this scope is bound to contain errors and omissions. If any reader should come across a mistake, I would appreciate if it were brought to my attention, such that it could be corrected in the next edition. Please feel free to e-mail me at: *indianwineguide@yahoo.co.in*. I am open to any ideas and suggestions for the improvement of this work.

Dr Aakash Singh Rathore
December 2005
New Delhi, India

PREFACE

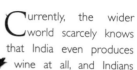

Currently, the wider world scarcely knows that India even produces wine at all, and Indians themselves are equally unaware that their country is slowly but surely becoming a top-class wine producer. There are currently no fewer than 75 types of wine produced by 20 major domestic wine production companies throughout India—in Maharashtra, Goa, Pondicherry, Bangalore, and Himachal Pradesh. As some know, an Indian sparkling wine, Omar Khayyam by Chateau Indage, has even won international awards. As the quality of domestic wines continues to increase in proportion to the ambition of India's new generation of winemakers, more international awards are on this side of the horizon.

And yet, there is currently not a single book treating the subject of Indian wine. The wine industry in India is booming. However, unless there is greater awareness among Indian wine drinkers (and potential wine drinkers) about the wide spectrum available with respect to high-quality domestic wines, Indians are going to continue to hunt for foreign supply, which is (mistakenly) regarded as better and more prestigious. And on the flip side, unless the wider world is made aware of the ever-growing number of quality wines coming out of India, the export of Indian wines will forever remain limited to supplying Indian restaurants abroad—a tiny, specialized market, much smaller than the industry's actual potential.

This book aims to contribute to the wider awareness of high-quality Indian wines, even as it guides the Indian consumer through all the brands, domestic and imported, on the Indian market. As with any wine guide (and every wine-producing country has one; major countries have dozens or even hundreds), The Complete Indian Wine Guide is surely going to pique your interest in wine, and I hope particularly in Indian wine. Indian wine, if properly supported and urged on, has a glorious future ahead.

This book will also help you as a consumer to choose the right wine for the right occasion, providing you with helpful information, and anecdotal material to share, display, and discuss when serving and enjoying wine.

Let me give you a brief outline of how this book is organized, so you can go directly to the material that interests you most.

Although the book is designed to be read straight through from beginning to end, it also functions as a work of reference. Thus, the chapters can easily stand independent of each other.

The **Introduction** gives a brief history of the presence of wine in India, up to the current wine boom, and offers some predictions with respect to the optimistic outlook for the future of Indian wines.

Part One includes how to taste wine, debunking certain myths about wine that scare away beginners, wine and food pairing, and other similar information. This part includes a thorough instruction on wine basics, such as storage, serving, glasses, and so on.

Part Two is the main part of the book, and it is what makes this book unique. There are several wine books available to anyone interested in wine, but none yet written for Indians. This book provides a comprehensive exposition of all domestic wines. Every single type of wine currently made and sold in India is tasted and reviewed, giving a description and ultimately an evaluation that will help consumers select the wines that sound best for them. The book covers the 2005, 2004 and 2003 vintages, and of course all non-vintage wines.

Part Three It presents an overview of international wines in general, and then focuses primarily on international wines regularly available on the Indian market. The international wines on the Indian market are of various types: so-called 'global joint ventures', that is, imported wines bottled by domestic producers in India; then there are those wines imported and marketed by domestic producers; and, finally, there are those wines imported by the foreign producers themselves. All the imported wines that are readily available on the Indian market will also be tasted and evaluated.

Finally, there are two Appendices designed to give special help to those who are beginners to wine appreciation. The first consists of a series of charts which list India's best wines—the best red, white, rosé, and sparkling; the best value wines; the best wine of each varietal (type of grape); and so on. The second Appendix provides a glossary of the technical terms used throughout the book, incorporating a pronunciation guide for unfamiliar foreign words and phrases.

INTRODUCTION

The Chequered History, Booming Present, and Promising Future of Indian Wine

Wine has a history in India, but it has never taken centre stage as it did at times in Europe. Wine is ensconced in western culture from ancient times (for example, Homer's epics, the first great literature of western civilization, repeatedly employ the phrase 'over the wine-dark sea'…). In India, wine was introduced by the various waves of conquerors and sojourners. Some people suggest that ancient India had an indigenous wine linked with mainstream religious rites and thus with general culture, but I do not believe that *soma*, the ancient gods' intoxicant, had anything to do with wine, that is, wine made from grapes.

One of the names for wine in ancient India was *Drakshasava*. Artefacts from Harappan civilization indicate familiarity with wine, though it is not known how much was produced or how much was generally consumed. Moving to the Vedic period, it is claimed that wine was known as *somarasa*, associated with Indra and poured as a libation and drunk at religious festivals. I doubt this was wine, and most scholars agree that it was most likely a product derivative of the mushroom, not the grape. But there were certainly some references and uses of wine before Alexander brought vines with him to northern India. For example, it is believed that pre-Alexander Shaivite cultic practices—in this sense analogous to Greek Bacchic rites—involved the use of wine as an intoxicant.

Kautilya's *Arthashastra*, which dates from somewhere between 321-150 BC discusses 'alcoholic beverages made from fruit', though it is not clear that wine proper was meant. Interestingly, the Mauryas strictly regulated the production and distribution of alcoholic beverages, and in this respect, the current outrageously

over-regulated Indian laws have a native predecessor.

The Persians had a famous wine, Shiraz, which was often sent to the Indian subcontinent for consumption by the Mughals, and later by the British. When in the eighteenth century political crises in Persia prevented shipments of Shiraz to India, the void was filled by shipments of Madeira brought in by East India Company vessels themselves.

From the moment the British set up the Surat factory (1612), wine became more and more familiar throughout India. Indeed, the breakfast given to all the employees at the Surat factory consisted of little else but 'burnt wine', that is, wine that was scalded by dropping a red hot brick of gold into it.

Wine was always expensive in India, and today is no different. Due to the cost of shipping wine to India, the British planted vineyards in Surat and Kashmir. Kashmir happens to fall right into the longitude (30°-50°) where the world's best wines originate, including California and Europe in the Northern Hemisphere, and Chile, South Africa, and Australia in the Southern Hemisphere. This suggests that if the Kashmir problem is ever solved, the wine problem in India will also be solved.

Some of the domestics were drinkable, in spite of the fact that viticulture was hardly known to India. As the production was picking up, in the nineteenth century a Phylloxera epidemic destroyed all the vines in India, just as it had done in Europe. While Europe replanted with resistant (American) root stocks grafted on to superior European vines, India did not. Thus, from the British landing in Surat in 1608 to today, the vast majority of the wine drunk in India has been imported.

And the wine the British drank was not just any import, but often some of the best. They developed the art of pairing Indian food and wine, although since the taste of wine has changed so much in the last century, it is difficult to agree now with their judgments. For example, Bordeaux Lafite or La Rosé was matched with Bombay Duck. Today this pairing would clearly be contraindicated.

In fact, because of the nonavailability of pure drinking water, the British drank an enormous amount of wine while in India, far more than they ever would at home. The record book of a British civilian resident in India, a certain Mr Francis, dated 1774, shows that in a single month his household consumed 75 bottles of Madeira, 99 bottles of claret (red Bordeaux), 74 bottles of porter (a stout beer), 16 bottles of rum, three bottles of brandy, and one bottle of cherry brandy!

Wine, then, got its deepest and widest instantiation in India during British rule. To give a brief summary of changing drinking patterns during the British Raj, one could basically say that from the 1600s to about 1820, wine was pre-eminently the drink of choice. Those who could not afford it had arrack (a spirit like toddy) or other indigenous spirits, but anyone of means had steady supplies of both domestic and imported wines ready at table. When the supply of imported wines was interrupted and/or domestic production was not of decent enough quality to drink, unadulterated punch was the substitute. Indeed, punch became the rage both in India and abroad during the seventeenth century. The Portuguese in India were crazy about it, and established several punch houses in Goa. The idea spread to Calcutta and Madras too. But this went out of fashion in India from around the 1750s, though the fad lasted another half-century in Britain itself.

The word *punch*, of course, derives from the Sanskrit-based Hindi word for five, *panch*: punch was an Indian concoction over 2000 years old consisting of five ingredients: arrack, sugar, lime juice, water, and spices (including clove, and other aromatics like rose water). The Europeans in India developed dozens of popular punches, one of which is still common today in British taverns, called East India Punch, a mixture of brandy, port, sugar, lime juice, and spices; the more festive, fizzy punch includes sparkling wine.

After the end of the punch fad by the 1750s, Persian Shiraz was regularly supplied to India. As already mentioned, this ended with political conflicts in Persia in the eighteenth century, and Persian Shiraz was substituted by Madeira—the only wine thought to improve, rather than deteriorate, in the torrid Indian climate.

With the invention of Indian pale ale, beer began to overtake wine consumption in India in the 1820s, and then from around 1840-1870, brandy began to be recognized as the drink of choice. At the same time, with soda becoming widely accessible, whisky became a strong contender. Additionally, around the 1860s, when the Schweppes company began marketing its anti-malaria tonic, gin began to gain currency as the best means for making tonic palatable. Finally, in the 1920s to 1930s, cocktails became a fad worldwide, and even today in

India, cocktails, whisky soda, rum, and brandy are far more widely consumed than wine.

Nevertheless, wine consumption in India is currently increasing at a rate of over 20 per cent per year and certain domestic wineries yearly sell out their entire stock. The best cannot keep pace with demand. Indeed, it is expected that wine consumption in India will grow tenfold to reach an average consumption of about 60 million bottles in the next 7-10 years.

Vineyards are multiplying in Maharashtra. Nashik is the current centre of the boom. Enterprising table grape farmers have shifted to growing wine-grape varieties, with generous subsidies from the state government. The

government of Maharashtra has issued over 70 licences in the last couple of years for setting up new wineries.

Further, the state's revenue department has introduced a zero excise duty regime with 4 per cent sales tax on locally produced wines. This is the most progressive action taken on the Indian wine scene, and hopefully other states will follow Maharashtra's lead.

Wine has a chequered history in India, but it also has a booming present. That is beyond dispute. And the present boom is occurring in spite of some of the most restrictive and, I dare say, regressive laws covering wine import, marketing, sales, and so on, in the world. As and when the market (and, naturally, Indian society) liberalizes, the stage is set for a glorious future. There is, however, one shadow hanging over this prediction, and that is the mistaken belief that Indian wine will never be on a par with international standards. That is, as the market liberalizes and more and more foreign brands are readily available, there is a ponderous threat that people will simply eschew Indian wines and lap up the foreign goods.

It need not be so. Provided that the Indian producers continue to attend to quality at least as diligently as they have been for the last two years, and preferably even more so. For if they can manage this, then the local product will be inherently competitive with the foreign rivals. It will then come down to questions of prejudice and conspicuous consumption, and these super-structural challenges may be faced by intelligent marketing and tactical distribution.

This introduction has got somewhat ahead of itself, insofar as inherent quality has been mentioned, as well as distinctions between table grapes and wine grapes and so on. Let us, then, turn to an exposition of exactly what wine is, and why it is so special. We shall now treat this subject and all its ancillary themes in Part One.

WINE BASICS
WHAT WINE IS AND HOW TO APPRECIATE IT

First and foremost, wine should be enjoyable in every way. By the time you finish reading this book, you will be very well informed about the wonderful world of wine and this will ensure that your experiences with wine may always be enjoyable. You will be able to buy wine with utmost confidence from any shop anywhere in the world, and you will be able to face the sommelier of any restaurant, howsoever grand and swanky, with however many stars, and ask without any hesitation for your choice of wine or for his informed recommendation. Gone will be the days of enophobia, or fear of wine.

Since I have just suggested that you will soon be able to consider yourself an aficionado, you might be surprised to hear me state now that learning the secrets and mysteries of wine history, production, geography, tasting, and so on, takes as much time as learning any other science or art. A typical enology (study of wine) course at university ranges from 4-year BAs to 2-year MAs and 6-year PhDs. Indeed, to earn the prestigious Wine Master title from the IMWEP in London can take you up to 20 years! Obviously, then, we are not going to go into all the fineries and minutiae here. Rather, we will distil all the essentials for you to comfortably read in a few sittings, and then refer back to later as your knowledge and experience continue to grow. You will be in complete control of all the essentials of wine, except that you will not necessarily be able to produce it.

When it comes to mastering wine, experience is the key. And let me assure you, just as the joy of drinking wine greatly surpasses the pleasure of writing about it, you will enjoy and learn far more about wine by drinking it rather than reading about it.

The cost of wine in India is admittedly quite prohibitive (unlike in many European countries, where wine costs less than water), but there are some less expensive domestic brands where you can begin.

Start with the wines of notable producers such as Sula, Grover, and Indage (or go through Part Two and get all the details, or turn to the Appendix and find the best wine values in India, and acquire those).

The Three Steps of
WINE TASTING

Anyone can drink wine just as anyone can look at a great painting, but to really taste wine, to appreciate it as one does a work of art, requires paying some attention. While wine is in a way simply a beverage, it also shares several important characteristics with art: it is often crafted with great personal care and can be the product of years of sweat and tears.

While learning to appreciate wine requires paying some attention, it does not require much effort or expense. Indeed, as there are basically only three steps to wine appreciation, we might say that getting maximum enjoyment out of a glass of wine is as easy as one, two, three.

THE EYE

The eye is the first organ used in the tasting of wine. It is rare, nowadays, to find wines possessing faults that can be spotted by the eye alone, but the visual inspection does give you key information about a wine's characteristics and quality. All wine tasting takes into account the appearance of the 'disc', the 'robe', and the 'legs' of a glass of wine.

The Disc

The disc is the upper surface of the wine in the glass. Look at it from above and from the side. The disc surface should be free of dust, debris or other solid matter, although you may occasionally find tiny pieces of cork if the bottle was not opened properly. The cork is completely harmless, but if the disc as a whole is matte, appearing dull and thick, this is almost certainly an indication that the wine is 'sick' with a microbe ailment. The more floating objects on the disc, the more 'dubious' the wine—approach it with caution. Deposits on the bottom of the glass, however, are not serious. These can be tannin (bitter grape-skin residues) or harmless tartrates.

After you have examined the disc of a wine, you might call it *limpid*, *bright* or *brilliant*, all terms denoting praise, or, on the other hand, *dubious*, *hazy*, *murky*.

The Robe

The robe is the colour of the wine. This is judged on the specific hue, and the intensity of that hue. The hue of white wines range from light yellow to bronze, and white wines darken (becoming brown) as they age. Reds range from violet and cherry red to deep purple, dark garnet, to almost black, and reds become lighter (becoming almost orange) as they age.

The colour of a white wine is often described as yellow, or pale yellow, or yellow gold, or, getting darker, bronze or pale bronze, and so on. A rosé is often termed grey, light red, salmon, or onion skin. A red is called light, garnet, ruby, and a younger one purplish, or older ones orangeish. Once you have spotted the general hue of a wine, then notice the intensity of the hue. For example, if it is a ruby-looking red, is it a deep, intense ruby, or a light, watery one? People refer to the intensity of a wine's colour with words like *deep, dense, rich*, or in contrast, *light, weak, poor*. In sum, you might look at the disc and robe of a good-quality young red wine and observe that it has a clear, bright disc free of 'floaters', and a deep purple robe.

The Legs

The third part of the visual examination of a glass of wine is to look at its 'legs', or 'tears'. Incline your glass or make a circular movement with your glass so that the wine rises and then runs back down the inner walls of the glass. As the wine runs back down, you will see teary-looking streams of clear liquid trickle more slowly down the sides of the glass. These are the legs. Actually, a wine's legs, while attractive, tell one next to nothing about the quality of a wine. A wine should form legs, and if it does not, then it is too low in extract (that is, glycerol, residual sugar, and other flavour compounds) or alcohol. But if it does, and most surely it will, that does not guarantee a good wine.

To sum up step one, realize that the eye of a wine will not only tell you whether your wine is red, white, or rosé, and not only if the wine may be sick or too weak, but it will also tell you whether it is bubbly or not. Sparkling wine (known popularly as Champagne) is also more a matter of eye than, for example, nose.

THE NOSE

The nose, like the eye of a wine, is also broken down into three aspects: the primary aromas, the secondary aromas and, the tertiary aromas. Before moving on to the primary aroma, you should know that there is also something called 'the first nose', which does not refer to the primary aromas. The first nose means that you smell a wine as soon as it has been poured out from the bottle. This quick sniff will immediately alert you to any problems with the wine, like any parasitic odours or strong chemicals e.g., sulphur dioxide (SO_2 smells like a burnt match, or at times worse, like a rotten egg) which indicate that the wine is foul. But if you do not smell anything terrible in the first nose, then continue to examine its aromas.

The olfactory examination of a glass of wine begins with a famous, or infamous, action: the wine taster grabs the wine glass by the foot of the stem and starts to swivel it so the wine swirls round and round in the glass. This is done in order to oxygenate the liquid, or 'let it breathe', which lets the unattractive chemicals like SO_2 clear out and opens up the aromatic qualities of a wine. Although real wine tasters tend to stick their noses deep into the wine glass, better manners are usually expected from the rest of us. Best thing, then, is to swirl the glass of wine as described and then raise it up to just below your nose.

The primary aromas are the fruity qualities coming from the grape itself. Each variety of grape, just like each fruit itself, has its own aromatic qualities. As you can imagine, it is extremely difficult to say, for example, what a mango smells like, or what a green apple smells like, but everyone pretty much knows what you mean when you say, 'that smells like a mango'. So, with a particular grape variety, one generally says that it smells like strawberries, or like cherries, like lychees, and so on. Concentrate on what you are smelling in the glass and you will notice that within the

complicated aroma of a glass of wine you can smell something fruity and that this fruit smell will remind you of the smell of some other fruit. Finding this fruit smell (often there is more than one, like cherry and strawberry both) is what it means to notice the primary aromas.

While the primary aromas spring out of the kind of grape itself, the secondary aromas are those which refer more to the wine as a whole. They result from the process of fermentation, and thus take into account not only the kind of grape(s), but also the yeast, the acids, the seeds, and stems, and all sorts of other aspects of turning grape juice into wine. The tertiary aromas, then, originate in the wine-ageing process, where you can smell the wood from the wine barrels and other aromas that come from the slight oxidation that occurs while a wine ages.

The primary aromas are thus more fruity, and are described as smelling like blackcurrant, raspberry, cherry, plum, and so on. The tertiary aromas tend to be more woody or resin-like (oak, pine, cedar, vanilla, smokey) and chemical-like (sulphur, acetone). But the secondary aromas have a huge range of possibilities, and in identifying these, wine tasters generally metamorphose into romantic poets.

Common aromas identified in different wines are spicy (clove, pepper, liquorice, ginger), floral (violet, rose, jasmine, acacia), vegetable-like (mushroom, capsicum), or mineral-like (chalk, flint). Domestic Indian wines often have domestic spicy aromas.

But are these smells really there in the wine, or are they in the wine taster's head? Laboratory tests seeking to answer this question have shown that fruits and flowers and the like tend to share a wide range of chemicals, but to be dominated by a particular compound or set of compounds—one set for oranges, which make them smell like oranges, one set for mangoes, making mangoes smell like mangoes, and so on. Wine, ultimately originating in grapes, but supplemented by several other ingredients such as yeast, oak, etc., also contains these chemical compounds, and some stand out more than the others. Thus, a wine may smell a bit like oranges if the dominant (odourous) chemical compound in oranges should be present in high concentrations in the wine.

THE MOUTH

Finally we have come to the point where one is most inclined to immediately put the wine, in the mouth. Be warned: gulping down wine without familiarizing oneself with its qualities can be seen by some as crude or unrefined. But here we are finally, at the mouth, or the taste of a wine.

The tongue distinguishes sweet, salty, acid, and bitter tastes. These tastes are complemented by 'touch' sensations in the oral cavity: feelings of heat and temperature, consistency (watery and fluid, or rich and viscous), and chemistry (such as astringency and gas). Thus, once the wine is in the mouth, you will be able to determine if it is too sweet or just right, if it is too acidic or nice and lively tasting, if it is too bitter or strong and firm tasting, or if the wine actually tastes salty, which can happen when the mineral flavours do not get balanced out by the wine's sugars and acids.

In addition to these tastes, there is the 'mouth feel'. The wine may feel hot and spicy, or it may feel cool—and notice that two wines served at the exact same physical temperature may have either one of these contrasting 'feels'. The wine may dry up your mouth from the tannin (the bitter element found on grape skins and present in wine). Or a wine may make your mouth pucker up from the acids. It may feel sticky from the excessive sugar. Or, what is best, it may actually feel balanced and harmonious, a result of all the elements of a wine complementing each other to produce a high-quality, delicious product.

One, Two, Three: eye, nose, mouth, or see, smell, taste. That is all there is to it. Most practiced tasters do the three steps almost simultaneously. And as you practise learning how to taste, i.e., appreciate a wine, you will find that the great amount of enjoymentthat results from the small investment of attention is very well worth the time.

Wine
AND HEALTH

The first thing that you should know with respect to the topic *wine and health* is that most people who know anything about wine believe that wine is good for you. Indeed, the great American founding father, Thomas Jefferson, sought to introduce European wine into the United States for its health benefits, and to dissuade

American consumption of unhealthy harder spirits like whisky, which he called 'the bane of America'. Contemporary science corroborates the traditional belief in the beneficial properties of wine.

In 1786, the English Doctor Herbeden had already noted that wine relieved the pain of patients suffering from angina pectoris. In 1974, research initiated by American cardiologists studying over 100,000 people, indicated that the risk of death from coronary diseases (notably myocardium infarct) was lower for moderate consumers of wine than for people who did not drink wine at all.

In case you have never heard of it, myocardium infarct occurs when the cardiac muscle is deprived of oxygenated blood—coronary arteries, providing blood, are obstructed or blocked up. Cholesterol is the principal factor responsible for this. And one solution is apparently wine.

The School of Public Health at Harvard calculated that the risk of heart disease was reduced by 45 per cent for people drinking one or two glasses of wine a day. In 1979, France and Italy, the largest consumers of wine, registered five times fewer deaths due to myocardium infarct than the US. Further, between 1952 and 1978 consumption of wine in the USA rose by 52 per cent and at the same time, death due to myocardium infarct fell by 22 per cent.

According to another study, for an equal consumption the risk of death by myocardium infarct is 1.03 per cent for beer drinkers, 1 per cent for spirit drinkers, and only 0.47 per cent for wine drinkers.

Moving away from the heart, moderate drinkers of wine are less prone to stress, cerebral thrombosis, rheumatoid arthritis, late-onset diabetes, Alzheimer's, and gallstones. With two glasses of red wine a day, you are 33 per cent less likely to get gallstones than people who do not drink wine.

The National Academy of Sciences published an article stating that moderate wine drinkers have greater protection against food-borne bacteria such as salmonella and e-coli, and that we have an 85 per cent greater resistance against one of five strains of the common cold virus.

If that is not enough, moderate wine drinkers are also likely to live two to five years longer than non-drinkers. And I should add that those wine drinkers who do not live longer, at least enjoy their short lifespan more intensely.

I am not urging you to drink wine. The facts speak for themselves.

What
WINE IS

Leaving aside the health benefits of wine, let us turn to wine itself. Everyone already knows that wine is simply fermented grape  juice. I do not want to go into the details of what fermentation is, because that is not going to prove terribly helpful for what we are trying to achieve; i.e., mastery of the basics of wine appreciation. It is enough to know that fermentation is the process by which grape juice becomes wine. It is popularly depicted by the following scheme:

SUGAR + YEAST = ALCOHOL + CARBON DIOXIDE

Sugar is naturally present in ripe grapes. Yeast is also usually present on grape skins, although it must be noted that wild yeasts are normally not used in modern winemaking, but rather special strains of yeast are added to the grape juice such that fermentation occurs in a more controlled manner, and the resulting wine is more a product of design than chance. The natural fermentation process ends when all the sugar present in the grape juice is converted into alcohol, or until the alcohol level in the grape juice (known in this process as 'must') reaches a percentage that makes the must toxic for the survival of the yeasts—about 15 per cent. The carbon dioxide that results from the process of fermentation escapes into the atmosphere; however, in the case of sparkling wine, such as Champagne, the carbon dioxide is trapped in the bottle, and that is what gives it the fizz.

The most general styles of wine is the oldest and still most popular: red wine. Red wine is made from black grapes (which are actually more often purplish or red) that are fermented with the skin, the seeds, and sometimes the stems. Red-wine styles range from light and refreshing to sweet and fortified, that is, with extra alcohol added. But all red wine has tannin, which can taste bitter. Tannin is found in the grape skins, seeds, and to some extent in stems. It is also present in the oak of barrels used to store and age wine.

Tannin is also present in tea which is responsible for making the tea bitter and leaving a dark ring around the tea cup. We break the tannin down in tea by adding milk; just so, you will often find people serve cheese with wine, as this helps to ease the bitterness of wine tannin. Tannin is an essential part of any red wine, but is less present in wines of lighter colour, since colour is a result of the contact of grape juice (which is colourless) with the grape skins.

Those who do not like the bitter element of red wine often prefer to drink rosé or white wines. But red wine is the most basic and still the most widely consumed type of wine.

Red wine is the only alcoholic beverage that can create itself. Human mediation is not necessary, since wild yeasts on the grape skins can seep into the grape and, given certain climactic conditions, fermentation can begin right there within the grape itself. Fermented grape juice is wine—thus, wine can make itself right there within one grape on a vine. This distinguishes wine, making it appear a most natural drink, and it has, for this and other reasons, historically been considered a gift from the gods.

Rosé wine is usually produced from black grapes without the stems. The juice is separated as soon as it is coloured sufficiently pink from the reddish-black grape skins. Styles vary enormously, as does the colour, ranging from pinks and oranges to greys, depending on the amount of time the juice remains in contact with the skins, and on the type of grape, each of which imparts a different hue.

This is the way serious rosé wine is made. There are, however, other ways. For example, the simplest process is to blend together some red wine with some white wine until the rosé colour is reached. This is called 'post-production blending', and is the most common method employed in India at present.

Surprisingly, white wine can be made from white or black grapes, since grape juice is generally colourless. As you may have expected, white grapes are not white—far from it. They can be pinkish, yellowish, golden, green, and so on, but are always far lighter in colour and far less tannic than black grapes. White wine styles vary from bone dry (that is, without any sweetness) to golden sweet, and are best when the acids from the wine balance with the alcohol and sugars. While red wine has to balance tannin, acids, alcohol, and sugars, white wine, since it has little to no tannin, has only to balance the other aspects.

Sparkling wine, to oversimplify it, is made when a yeast and sugar solution is added to normal wine and the wine undergoes fermentation in the bottle, where the carbon dioxide is trapped. When the bottle is opened, the gas seeps out, creating the fizz.

Sparkling wine is made in many countries, but the most famous is Champagne of France.

There are other ways of making sparkling wine. People generally regard the Champagne method as the best, although some argue that equally good wine could possibly be made without fermentation in the bottle, but instead in covered vats, with the sparkling wine pumped under pressure into bottles.

These are the basic types of wine. You can tell which one of these a wine is by just looking at it. If it is red, it is a red wine; if it bubbles, it is a sparkling wine, and so on. But how do you know what it will taste like?

Generally, the grape variety is the best indication of what the wine will taste like. Different grapes have different flavours and aromas, and thus you can usually expect a Cabernet (this is a grape variety, explained below) to taste one way and a Riesling (another grape variety) to taste another way, even if they have been made in France, USA, or Australia. Listed below are the most common grape varieties and the flavours commonly associated with them.

The origin of the wine is the next best indicator of taste. Many European wines (most notably France) do not state the grape varieties on the label, so you can predict what the grape variety will be by knowing what variety is used in the region listed on the label. This is not as complicated as it may sound. You will see how this is done when we get to the different regions in Part Three.

Another factor determining what to expect in a bottle of wine is called the vintage. The word 'vintage' is often bandied around to denote something special. It simply refers to wine from a particular year. So, wine made in the year 2000 is a '2000 vintage'.

These basic indicators of taste tell us that we need to look at grape varieties and at regions in order to know something about wine. Vintage is definitely an advanced issue, and very few people who are not connoisseurs of wine know anything about vintage. Even connoisseurs tend simply to carry a card around with them that lists all the best vintages for the various regions, and these can be picked up in any good wine store.

Grape varieties, though, are widely known, at least by name, if not by taste. Everyone would have heard names like Riesling, Cabernet Sauvignon (called Cab-Sav by enophiles, or wine lovers), and Chardonnay. These are the most commonly ordered and discussed wines at restaurants and parties around the world.

On most wine bottles you will find the name of the grape either on the front label or on the back label. If you do not find it anywhere, then you are stuck either trying to figure out which

RED-WINE GRAPES
(Also called Black Grapes)

CABERNET SAUVIGNON is the noblest of all red grapes. No matter where it is made, it tends to have a distinctive blackcurrant flavour, often with a hint of mint and cedar.

MERLOT is a variety often blended with Cabernet Sauvignon. It makes a juicy wine, with fruity flavours of blackcurrant, black cherry, and often mint. It is velvety, and low in tannic bitterness and higher in alcohol than Cabernet Sauvignon.

PINOT NOIR is another very famous black grape. It has a much thinner skin than Cabernet Sauvignon, and thus imparts much less tannin into the wine. Flavours commonly associated with it are raspberry and strawberry, often with a hint of game.

GAMAY is generally not considered the finest of grapes, but it does form the main ingredient to the very famous Beaujolais wines. It has cherry and candy flavours, with a hint of raspberry. To me it often tastes like jam or preserves. It makes light, fruity red wines.

SYRAH, also known as Shiraz, results in an intense and complex wine with sweet fruit flavours, particularly blackberry and raspberry, with a peppery overtone.

ZINFANDEL is found only in America and now in India. It can produce light and elegant white or rosé wines, but the most well-known red wines tend to be very big (that is, high in alcohol, also called full and rich) and tannic. In all styles the Zinfandel berry character is easy to identify.

There are numerous other near-major varieties of importance, such as Nebbiolo, Tempranillo, Sangiovese, etc., and then countless lesser-known varieties. The most important varieties that are not described above can be found in Appendix 2 (Glossary).

WHITE GRAPES
(Used for Both Red & White Wines)

CHARDONNAY is the king of white grapes. It always tends to have a buttery taste, and often a lemony and sometimes nutty flavours. The grape grown in warmer climates tends to have a strong hint of tropical fruit.

RIESLING makes light-bodied wines low in alcohol. They tend to be zesty and the fine ones often have a strong aroma of lychee.

SAUVIGNON BLANC is known for its sharp, tangy, gooseberry flavour. It may also have undertones of grass and asparagus. This grape has met with the highest success in India, producing flinty, tangy wines of character.

SEMILLON is a special grape as it is susceptible to what is called 'noble rot', or botrytis. That is a much-prized shrivelling up of the grape on the vine that leads to a wine that is high in sugar concentration and results in a delicious, sweet, honey-flavoured wine with hints of peaches and apricots. The dry wines coming from the not-rotted version of the grape has flavours of nectarine and lemon.

CHENIN BLANC should also be mentioned, if only because it is a major crop for domestic winemakers in India. In Europe, it is used for a range of wines including dry and sharp, sparkling, medium and extra sweet wines. Mature examples tend to have a nutty, honey-like flavour.

grapes were used by trying to smell and taste the peculiar characteristics of certain grape varieties, or you can deduce the grape varieties by noticing where the wine was made, which you will certainly find on either the front or back label. Trying to sniff and taste your way to the grape is often impossible given that wines can be made from blends of many different grapes, with no one type revealing its identifiable characteristics. Thus, either you just stop worrying about the grape and enjoy the wine, or you keep in mind which regions tend to use which grapes. This is described in Part Three.

Wine Etiquette
MOVING BEYOND THE MYTHS

Nowadays everyone seems to know something about wine, and far too many claim to know too much. This is partly a result of and partly a cause for the fact that the wine industry in India is beginning to boom. As mentioned already, sales are rising by some 20-25 per cent per year, with more varieties of wine available on the market now than ever before. There are wine tasting clubs in the metros as well as wine bars opening all around. The quality of domestic wine production is beginning to improve. And quite gradually, duties on wine are falling.

But there are still glitches in the wine boom. For example, those who know too much about wine (that is, those who think they know everything) are responsible for a fear of wine among many who only know little. There is widespread enophobia, a fear that to understand the complex world of wine requires erudition, or at the very least too much time and energy. But let me assure you that this fear is unfounded. It largely results from wine snobs' pantheon of myths. For example, it is a myth that one may only drink a certain type of wine when eating certain foods. On the contrary, most wines go pretty well with most foods. While indeed some styles of wine do go better with some foods, and a few wines go quite badly with a few foods, there are no sacred rules that must be strictly adhered to. Perhaps there is one: always drink what you like. After all, you only eat what you like, don't you?

Pairing
FOOD AND WINE

Pairing food and wine is not an esoteric science. When you are selecting a wine to match your meal, just choose a wine that you would want to drink by itself. You will probably drink most of the wine without the food—either before the food is served or after you have finished eating. Therefore, even if the pairing is not perfect, you will not go wrong if you make sure that both the food and the wine are good. The best approach is to experiment with different combinations and see what works for you.

If you need guidelines to begin with, then here are some sound ones. First, try to drink the wine of the region where the food is from. So, have Italian wine with pasta, Spanish wine with paella, southern French wines with Mediterranean food, Hungarian wine with goulash, Greek wine with a Greek salad, northern European wines with food from northern Europe, and so on. Of course, this poses special problems for Asian foods. Most people agree that with spicy Asian foods a cool, crisp white wine works best. Rieslings, Gewürztraminers, and Sauvignon Blancs are the recommended varietals especially for vegetarian meals. With spicy, light meat dishes, one might try lighter reds like those from Beaujolais or the Loire. Lambrusco, a fruity red sparkling wine from Italy, also pairs well with both vegetarian and non-vegetarian Indian food.

Second, if the regional approach is not suitable, then try the weight approach. Heavy, hearty food may require a hearty wine, because it will make a lighter wine taste insipid. Meats like beef and lamb can thus pair with heavy, deeply rich reds like Cabernets and Syrahs. With lighter food you have more options. Lighter wines (Chenin Blanc, white Bordeaux, Tavel, Pinot Noirs) will balance nicely, but you may also keep to heartier wines. Actually, heavy wines usually do not overpower light foods, despite what purists say.

Finally, here is a suggestion on how to avoid the most common mismatches. These tend to occur at the beginning or the end of a meal. With salads, the wine should be as dry and crisp as possible. On the other hand, when the food is sweet, then the wine should be sweeter. There are some famous dessert wines (Tokay, Sauternes, Eiswein) that pair very well with many desserts. However, most sweet dishes seem to throw dessert wines out of balance and accentuate their acidity rather than their sweetness. It may be best to have your dessert wine as a dessert rather than to serve it with dessert.

Again, the best way to decide which wines pair well with your favourite foods is to experiment. You will also want to experiment with the wines alone, to find out where your preferences lie. There are several essential world wines you must try. Let us start with the best whites: German and Australian Rieslings; Chenin Blanc; Chablis, Chardonnay; Sauvignon Blanc; and Gewürztraminer. The list of must-try red wines are: Beaujolais; Rioja; California Pinot Noir; Burgundy; Chianti; Bordeaux; American Merlot, and Zinfandel; Cabernet Sauvignons from the United States and Australia; Rhône wines like Chateau-Neuf-du-Pape; and, Australian Shiraz. If you would like to try a serious rosé, French Tavel is probably the best.

Storage
OF WINE

Storage of wine is also no mystery. If you plan to collect wines and store them at home, you need to be careful. Wine cellars, of course, are hard to come by. But long exposure to heat of over 20°C will certainly ruin your wine. Optimum storing temperature is 10-12°C, but any constant temperature within 5-18°C will do. Bottles will stay in fair condition stored on their side in a constantly air-conditioned room. If you cannot find a place that is cool enough, you may store your bottles in the warmest part of the refrigerator, but you need to be sure not to move and shake the bottles around too much. If you have a spare fridge, then you can transform it into a mini wine cellar by setting it to the lowest cooling temperature and readjusting the shelves to hold all the bottles on their sides.

Returning to myths about wine, other common ones are about decanting and about the glasses in which different wines must be served.

Serving
WINE

Serving wine should remain casual and enjoyable, not ritualistic and over formal. You will rarely run into a wine younger than 20 years old that really needs decanting. A bit of sediment in the bottom of a glass never killed anyone. Most decanting is done solely to look good. And this also explains the different sizes of glasses in which red and white wines are served. There is no real reason that white wine should be served in a smaller glass than red—it is just for looks. There is certainly nothing wrong with presenting a nice wine in a pretty decanter and pouring out the different wines in different glasses, but you should not feel that this is how it has to be done and fear doing it wrong.

In each region in the old world where wine is produced (Germany, France, Spain, Italy, etc.), a local glass is used, different not only from those of other regions, but also different from the standard international five-star hotel wine glasses. Anyone, therefore, who tells you that a German Riesling must be served in a white wine glass is simply being officious. To antagonize such people, I serve Beaujolais in steel cups, reason being that Beaujolais is vinified in steel vats. But to be serious, as long as your glasses are clean and clear and are filled less than two-thirds so that the aroma of the wine can fill the rest of the space, then they are perfectly fine. There is nothing to fear in the presentation or service of wines, as long as the wine itself is good.

So shake off any fears you may have had about wines and join in the wine boom underway. Try the essential wines that are listed, store them and serve them however convenient. Try pairing your wines with those foods suggested, and experiment with different wines and different combinations. Also, try some Indian domestic wines (with Indian food), because these are only going to improve if consumers make demands for higher quality. In a few years, the list of must-try world wines might even include some domestic— perhaps in a unique Indian glass?

FOOD	WHITE WINE	RED WINE
Fish, shellfish in light sauces, light cutlets, ham, light cheeses, tacos, salads, light Japanese food, light omelettes, appetizers (samosas, pakoras)	Soave, Orvieto, Pinot Grigio, Riesling, Muscadet, Champagne and other dry sparkling wines, Chenin Blanc, French Chablis and other unoaked Chardonnays, Sauvignon Blanc	
Spicier fish, shellfish in heavier sauces, spicier or heavier egg dishes, pasta in light sauces, turkey, light veal, heavy or sharp cheeses, paneer dishes, enchiladas, spicy Chinese, Thai and Japanese food	White Bordeaux, White Burgundy, Pinot Gris, Gewürztraminer, oaked Chardonnay	Beaujolais, Lambrusco, Borgueil, Chinon
Heavy potato dishes, pasta with heavy sauces, pizzas, bacon, sausage and pork, rabbit, Asian foods prepared with heavy meats	Heavy (oaked) Chardonnay, Tavel (French rosé)	Valpolicella, Beaujolais, Dolcetto, Rioja, California Pinot Noir, Burgundy, Barbera, Chianti, Barbaresco
Lobster, beef, veal, broiled fish in heavy sauces, stewed lamb, wild game		Italian Barolo, Red Bordeaux, Merlot (USA), Zinfandel, Cabernet Sauvignon (USA, Australia), Rhône, Syrah/ Shiraz
Sweet dishes	Sautrnes, Hungarian Tokay, Late-harvest sweet wines (Australia, USA), German Auslese and Eiswein	Madeira or Porto

FOOD	WHITE WINE	RED WINE
Fish, shellfish in light sauces, light cutlets, ham, light cheeses, tacos, salads, light Japanese food, light omelettes, appetizers (samosas, pakoras)	Sula Brut, Marquis du Pompadour, N.D. Hoor, Vinsura Chenin Blanc, Flamingo Chenin Blanc, N.D. Sauvignon Blanc, Vinsura Sauvignon Blanc, Greno Sauvignon Blanc	
Spicier fish, shellfish in heavier sauces, spicier or heavier egg dishes, pasta in light sauces, turkey, light veal, heavy or sharp cheeses, paneer dishes, enchiladas, spicy Chinese, Thai and Japanese food	Grover Viognier, Indage Viognier, Bluefolds Sauvignon Blanc, Sula Rosé, Vinsura Rosé, Greno Chenin Blanc	Sailo Mark Antony
Heavy potato dishes, pasta with heavy sauces, pizzas, bacon, sausage and pork, rabbit, Asian foods prepared with heavy meats	Indage Ivy Chardonnay/Semillon, Bluefolds Chenin Blanc, Dajeebah Chardonnay	N.D. Cabernet Sauvignon, Vinsura Zinfandel, N.D. Cabernet/Shiraz, Bluefolds Syrah, Indage Ivy Malbec, Dajeebah Syrah, Saikripa Cabernet/Merlot
Lobster, beef, veal, broiled fish in heavy sauces, stewed lamb, wild game		Indage Ivy Shiraz, Flamingo Zinfandel, Grover Cabernet/Shiraz, Flamingo Cabernet/Shiraz, Dajeebah Merlot
Sweet dishes	[Presently, there is no proper Indian dessert wine. No Indian sweet wine or Port-styled wine is of sufficient quality to recommend.]	

Part II

COMPLETE GUIDE TO
DOMESTIC INDIAN WINES

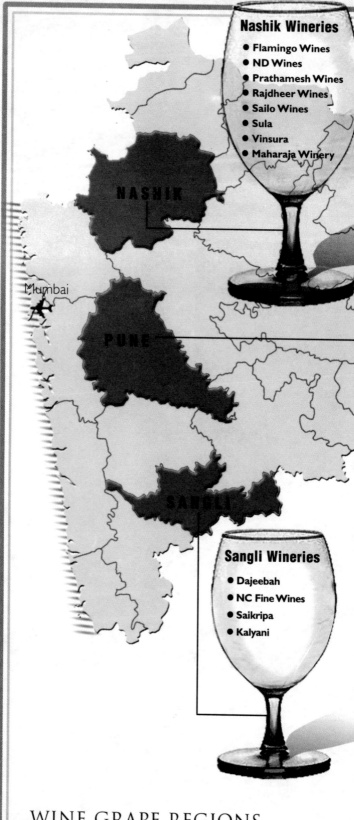

Nashik Wineries

- Flamingo Wines
- ND Wines
- Prathamesh Wines
- Rajdheer Wines
- Sailo Wines
- Sula
- Vinsura
- Maharaja Winery

NASHIK

Mumbai

PUNE

SANGLI

Sangli Wineries

- Dajeebah
- NC Fine Wines
- Saikripa
- Kalyani

WINE GRAPE REGIONS

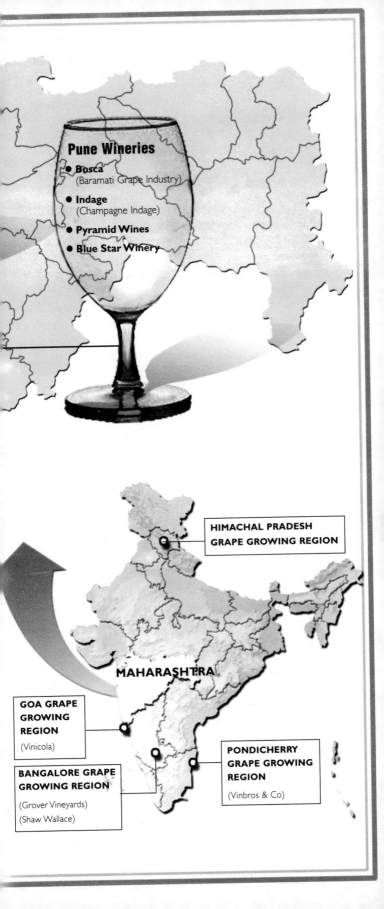

Pune Wineries

- **Bosca**
  (Baramati Grape Industry)

- **Indage**
  (Champagne Indage)

- **Pyramid Wines**

- **Blue Star Winery**

HIMACHAL PRADESH
GRAPE GROWING REGION

MAHARASHTRA

GOA GRAPE
GROWING
REGION

(Vinicola)

BANGALORE GRAPE
GROWING REGION

(Grover Vineyards)
(Shaw Wallace)

PONDICHERRY
GRAPE GROWING
REGION

(Vinbros & Co)

The domestic wine industry, along with consumption of imports is booming. The rapid expansion of domestic production is great news for those of us who love wine but suffer from the hefty prices imported wines command in India.

In mid 2005, there were no less than 20 good-sized producers of wine in India; 'good sized' being relative, of course. There are numerous other smaller producers, and indeed, I have observed that there are private individuals spread out all over the country trying their hand at producing wines in their own back gardens. But the major producers, listed in alphabetical order, are these:

- BLUEFOLDS (Blue Star Agro Winery)
- BOSCA (Baramati Grape Industries)
- DAJEEBAH WINES (Datacone Wine Industry)
- FLAMINGO WINES
- GRENO VINEYARDS (Greengold Wines)
- GROVER VINEYARDS
- INDAGE (Champagne Indage)
- N.C. FINE WINES
- N.D. WINES
- PRATHAMESH WINES
- PRINCESS (In-Vogue Creations)
- PYRAMID WINES
- RAJDHEER WINES
- SAIKRIPA WINERY (Saee Group)
- SAILO WINES (V.M. Agrosoft)
- SHAW WALLACE
- SULA VINEYARDS (Samant Soma Wines)
- VINBROS & CO.
- VINICOLA
- VINSURA (Sankalp Winery)

Some of these are bigger and better than others. This part of the book is devoted to exploring these domestic wine producers and, most importantly, the wines they produce. The wineries not on this list include Golden Agro from the Punjab, Sai Wineries from Panjim, Goa, and a handful of others, one from Himachal Pradesh, and the rest from Nashik, Sangli, and

Goa. The current condition of these wineries is so bad—either undeveloped or dilapidated— that there is not much point in discussing them in this edition of *The Complete Indian Wine Guide*. As it stands, as and when a bottle of wine gets produced by one of them, for example Golden Agro, it is hard to recognize the beverage as wine. Golden Agro's Royal Visa White Wine contains 17 per cent alcohol! The products of most of these alleged wineries are actually distilled. They are primarily whisky (or other spirit) distilleries that believe there is profit to be made in the current wine boom, and so have tried their hand at imitating wine.

There are also several other wineries not mentioned because they do not have wines available on the market yet. There is a list of a handful of such wineries at the end of Part Two. Presuming that these wineries attempt to make real wine, and not the sinister brews of the likes of Golden Agro, then any of their wines are worth keeping a watch for.

As for the wines discussed herein, I have personally tasted each and every one of them (unless otherwise noted), and have evaluated them as objectively and attentively as possible.

Evaluation
OF THE WINES

All the wines are tasted and described in accordance with the wine-tasting procedure outlined in Part One. I have given them a rating on a five-star scale based on their merits:

÷ **POOR**
÷÷ **AVERAGE**
÷÷÷ **GOOD**
÷÷÷÷ **VERY GOOD**
÷÷÷÷÷ **EXCELLENT**

I have tried to be as generous as possible, considering that wine production is still a fledgling industry in India, but I have never exaggerated, considering also that the reader should be soundly steered away from bad wines and led in the direction of the finer achievements.

The wines are evaluated with respect to their inherent qualit that is, their balance, elegance, and other objective factors th most wine specialists would readily and easily agree upo Additionally, I have kept in mind the wine's quality in relation t its price. This becomes explicit in the Appendix, where I hav listed the best wine values on the market, that is, the best wine you can buy at the lowest prices. This should help anyone who interested in trying Indian wine to go directly to the best valu wines currently available.

It should be noted that wines are given ratings in respect t other Indian wines. That means that EXCELLENT wines wou likely fall into the simply VERY GOOD category in comparisc with their more established international counterparts.

Similarly, AVERAGE domestic wines are probably POO international wines. But if you are just getting started in wir appreciation, these wines are certainly drinkable. They are neith good nor very bad, but passable.

BLUEFOLDS

(Blue Star Agro Winery)
50/2 Birdawadi, Ambethan Rd.,
Chakan, Pune, MS, 410 501

Bluefolds is actually one of the brand names of the company Blue Star. Blue Star currently sells the following wines:

1. Bluefolds Syrah
2. Bluefolds Chenin Blanc
3. Bluefolds Sauvignon Blanc
4. Evita Ruby Red Wine
5. Eldoro Red Wine

The last two wines are the cheapest, and do not really warrant attention. Eldoro is made from table grapes. The Bluefolds wines, on the other hand, do not just warrant attention, they command it. These are some of India's best wines. The big challenge for this up-and-coming winery will be to produce a 2005 vintage just as good as the 2004 one.

✦✦✦✦ BLUEFOLDS SYRAH (12.5%) 2004

EYE: Dark, grapy garnet robe with pink/purple edges.
NOSE: Cherry pits and strawberries with a hint of sweetness; very inviting nose.
TASTE: Good acid, mild but decent tannin, fairly full in the mouth, black pepper on the finish.

EVALUATION

The main problem with the wine is that it has insufficient body. Another issue is that some bottles seem to have a bit too much sulphur, but on the other hand, some bottles also have a pronounced touch of tobacco in the nose that is just lovely. All in all, considering that the wine is well priced at Rs. 350, it is VERY GOOD.

✦✦✦✦ BLUEFOLDS CHENIN BLANC (12.5%) 2004

EYE: Straw gold with green edge.
NOSE: Primarily peach and apricot nose with a touch of white raisins.
TASTE: Somewhat flabby and unstructured, but wonderfully abundant with fruit, peaches, and

cream, and an interesting sweet biscuit. Steel and copper on the finish.

EVALUATION:
>   VERY GOOD especially for a price as low as Rs. 330.

++++ BLUEFOLDS SAUVIGNON BLANC (12.5%) 2004

EYE: Watery edge, with a nearly transparent robe—if there is any colour to it, it is green gold.
NOSE: A bizarre mix of barley, beer and white grape.
TASTE: Tingly crisp acids, a lot of banana, and a hint of vanilla; a creamy coating in the mouth.

EVALUATION:
>   An Indian white wine with character. It is VERY GOOD, surely India's best and a steal at Rs. 330.

++ EVITA RUBY RED WINE (12.5%) 2004

EYE: Very watery edge, not terribly inspiring body, but at least clean looking.
NOSE: A lot of scented candle wax, green and spicy.
TASTE: Slightly sweet, it goes down easy, but it is far too watery and thin.

EVALUATION
>   The nose is the best feature of this low-cost wine. It is only Rs. 210, and nothing more than AVERAGE.

CONCLUSION

Blue Star has a high-tech winery with all new equipment imported from Italy. They have a 300,000 litre capacity, which they have only just begun to tap. They have produced something like 50,000 litres of good wine in 2004. Provided they can manage to open the market, they will increase their output year upon year. Again, the challenge for this winery is to ensure that each year the quality matches or supersedes that of 2004. If they can accomplish this, then Bluefolds will surely become one of India's premier wine brands.

BOSCA WINE

(Baramati Grape Industries)
P.O. Pimpali, Tal. Baramati
District Pune, MS, 413 102

Bosca Wines are possibly India's worst. It has a huge capacity of some 4.5 million litres. Thankfully only about 200,000 litres of wine are produced annually, the enterprise preferring to focus on the more profitable spirit production.

Bosca sells the following five wine (or wine-like) labels:

1. Sherry
2. Vermouth Torino
3. Riesling
4. Red Wine
5. Rosé Wine

The first two fall outside the scope of this book, as they are fortified wines, and not wines per se. That leaves the Riesling, the Red and Rosé wines.

÷ RIESLING (12.5%) 2002

EYE: Watery greenish gold.
NOSE: Foul, green, and alcoholized.
TASTE: Simply repulsive, not the remotest similarity to Riesling.

EVALUATION
POOR! The so-called Riesling does not have a single berry of Riesling in it. Indeed, the label (as crazy as the wine) indicates that Baramati grapes have been used, which means common table grapes, perhaps Thompson seedless or Ganesh.

÷ RED WINE (12%) 2002

EYE: Watery red brick.
NOSE: Sinister, terrible, maderized and alcoholized.
TASTE: Repulsive.

EVALUATION
POOR! I do not know which is worse, the labelling/bottling or the wine itself. The label

states 'BOSCA, in technical collaboration with Bosca, Italy'. And then 'ESTATE BOTTLED Red Wine'. It also includes that the wine is made from the finest Baramati grapes, which I suppose might be Bangalore Blue or something of that ilk.

✢ RED WINE 2002

There is really no point of going through the tasting process with this. It will be just as bad as the others, and I am afraid to try it just from the look of it.

CONCLUSION

Bosca is a tragedy. Although they have the means to improve their facilities and consequently their product, there is no will to make any improvements. The wines are sold to hotels and restaurants around the country as a cooking wine. Bosca uses local grapes, dirt cheap; ferment the concoction in cement tanks, probably extremely unhygienic, and use the appalling bottles and labels that match the horrific product. The wines cost only Rs. 125 each, but this is still Rs. 125 too much. It is an embarrassment to the Indian wine industry and all the more execrable that people associate the winery with the Union Agricultural Minister.

DAJEEBAH

271, Samrajya, Sangliwadi
Sangli, MS, 416416

Dajeebah is a relatively young enterprise but is now attempting to strengthen its line. It has an extremely attractive range of noble grape varieties planned for its line, but as of now are only producing limited volumes:

1. Cabernet Sauvignon
2. Merlot
3. Syrah (Shiraz)
4. Zinfandel
5. Sauvignon Blanc
6. Chardonnay

Dajeebah also has two easy-drinking blends, which is to say wines made from local, non-noble grape varieties:

7. Shherly Dry Red Wine
8. Balleee Sweet Red Wine

Dajeebah, in the Sangli district, is located in the Krishna Valley belt, in the Sahyadri Hills. It appears that the Sangli area has well drained soils which are not too fertile. Less fertile soils are usually an advantage for the production of high-quality wine grapes, as stressed vines produce a lesser quantity (and thus, generally higher quality) of berries. But Dajeebah has a battle on their hands, as it is growing a couple of varietals that have not flourished up to now in India, that is, Chardonnay and Merlot.

In 2003, Dajeebah crushed a little of everything, Cabernet Sauvignon, Zinfandel, Merlot, Syrah (Shiraz), Sauvignon Blanc, Chardonnay, and some Bangalore Purple for the jug wines (Shherly and Balleee).

In 2004, having already so much supply in chill, it went only for Sauvignon Blanc, and in 2005, only crushed Cabernet Sauvignon (and perhaps some Chenin Blanc, but I didn't identify it).

Most of the wines on the market now are, thus, actually 2003 vintage, although they would have been bottled (produced) in either 2004 or 2005. Fortunately for everyone, in 2006 Dajeebah will crush another magnificent panache of interesting, unique varietals.

As you may have gleaned from all the 'h's and 'e's, Dajeebah likes to overuse letters. This has come to haunt them on their labels, which all misspell the name of the company, Dajeebah Vineyards, as Dajeebah Vineyarrds. I say 'haunt them' because at first I had thought the incorrect spelling to be a mistake and wondered why the typo had not been caught before the wines were sent to the market. Later when visiting the winery I learned that the misspelling was not at all unintended, it is based on astrology. To each his own, as long as the wine is good!

Let us turn to an evaluation of the wines, and see if the wine is good enough to forgive them for their absurd decision to misspell everything on the labels.

⊹⊹ CABERNET SAUVIGNON (13%) LABELLED 2004

EYE: The colour is dark but not intense. The disc is nice and clear and the legs are prolific.

NOSE: Foxy, maderized and thin. There is a hint of plum over time, and a touch of wood (were oak chips added to the vat, or is it the stem?) is detectible.

TASTE: There is some tannin, which is nice for a change. The problem is that there is a lot of sherry-maderized flavour coming through, and the finish is astringent. There is unfortunately no complexity.

EVALUATION

The wine is AVERAGE. It is overpriced at Rs. 402, but I suppose Dajeebah would retort that making a 100 per cent Cabernet wine is an expensive undertaking.

✛✛✛✛ MERLOT (13%) LABELLED 2004

EYE: Light red with orange streaks, more brilliant than the other reds.
NOSE: Closed with too much sulphur. Maderized with overripe raspberries. Attractive Merlot character is present.
TASTE: Smooth, warm, dark-red fruit and a touch of spice (clove).

EVALUATION

This is the only Indian-made Merlot on the market! Too bad there are only 5000 bottles of it. The main problem with the wine is that it is a bit flabby, but in spite of this, if they keep the price as planned at Rs. 312, I would say it is VERY GOOD.

✛✛✛ SYRAH (13%) LABELLED 2004

EYE: Nice looking garnet, brilliant but very thin.
NOSE: Saline and mineral, slightly closed and green.
TASTE: Warm and rich, slight touch of raspberry sweetness and perfectly smooth tannin.

EVALUATION

I like the way they have gone for a Côte-du-Rhône style with this wine. It is not a great wine, of course, but at Rs. 384 it is GOOD.

✦✦ ZINFANDEL (13%) LABELLED 2004

EYE: Cloudy and thin with a watery edge.

NOSE: Strange resiny smell, but basically has the aroma of chlorinated tap water.

TASTE: It has got a damp, earthy punch to it, with very mild tannin.

EVALUATION

To be fair, there could be a problem with this bottle, because the wine is pretty disappointing, and that is out of sync with much of the Dajeebah line. What I have got in front of me costs Rs. 393 and is only AVERAGE.

✦✦✦ CHARDONNAY (13%) LABELLED 2004

EYE: A rich yellow straw of good intensity.

NOSE: Apple cider and cheddar cheese, a lovely hint of Chardonnay butter, and a touch of clove.

TASTE: Decent buttery coating, but overpowering cheesy lactic acids, and too much bitterness; the finish is nutty (pistachio).

EVALUATION

This is one of the only Indian-made Chardonnays on the market! It is a very good start with this varietal, and I look forward to following their progress with this label over the coming years. The price is not fixed yet, but their lower suggestion was Rs. 402, and I think this is okay, given the competition. I hope they resist their temptation to price it higher. GOOD.

✦✦ SAUVIGNON BLANC (13%) LABELLED 2004

EYE: A darker hue of gold than the Chardonnay. But far less rich.

NOSE: A honey aroma reminiscent of Hungarian Tokaj, also some corkyness.

TASTE: Thin, unattractive saliva-like watery-acid mix.

EVALUATION

This one is not a success. It is also expensive at Rs. 465. I hope the 2005 is better. This wine is AVERAGE.

✦ SHHERLY (14%) LABELLED 2004

EYE: Light and watery.
NOSE: Oxidized and closed, sour smell.
TASTE: Leathery, grapy, undeveloped and unattractively thin.

EVALUATION

The wine is POOR; I might have pushed it up to AVERAGE, but there are much better buys in the Rs. 200 range, so this one cannot be recommended.

✦ BALLEEE (14%) 2004

EYE: The unattractive robe of a typical red jug wine.
NOSE: Smells sickly sweet and highly alcoholic.
TASTE: Too sweet to taste anything else. Obviously chaptalized (that is, sugars added).

EVALUATION

For only about Rs. 125, I suppose it is as cheap as Indian wine gets. However, I still cannot judge it anything but POOR.

CONCLUSION

Dajeebah is off to a pretty good start. Keeping aside the lower end products, the premium wines of this growing winery have at least one very special feature: the only domestic Merlot. The Chardonnay is also a rarity. But they have a lot of work ahead, they need to improve their Cabernet Sauvignon, Zinfandel, and Sauvignon Blanc. If they manage this, their future is bright.

FLAMINGO WINES

C U 4, MIDC Vinchur, Tal. Niphad,
Dist. Nashik, 422 305, M.S.

Flamingo is one of the new wineries coming up in a wine park, in Maharashtra, that is, a government subsidized industrial area carved out in order to encourage domestic production of wine. Some of India's best wines coming up are now coming out of these places, and in the coming years, you will find more and more quality producers and, more importantly, quality wines originating in wine parks.

Flamingo is in the process of bottling and marketing its new line of wines, but I was able to taste them out of the vats at the high-tech winery near Nashik. The 2004 line includes the following varietals/blends:

1. Chenin Blanc
2. Sauvignon Blanc
3. Zinfandel
4. Cabernet-Shiraz

There is also going to be a Rosé, which will be a post-production blend of red and white wines—I tried to dissuade them from this deplorable practice, but they insisted that rosé wines were in big demand, and that the Indian palate had not developed enough to discern whether a rosé were post-blended or naturally produced. Flamingo's able enologist, Dilip J. Nevkar, may be right at present, but what he assumes will not hold true for long, and then they will find themselves in a fix.

Nevkar and I tasted the wines together, and discussed the successes and failures of Flamingo's product line. I got the distinct impression that he is serious about producing quality wine. They have a good deal of work ahead of them, but Flamingo is unquestionably a winery to watch.

✦✦✦ CHENIN BLANC (14%) 2004

EYE:
: Dull, tropical-looking light gold (note: the wine tasted had yet to be filtered, which would give the disc a brighter shine).

NOSE:
: Hit by a strange musky, overripe odour, and then a high (ethyl) alcohol blast which is disconnected or not integrated.

TASTE:
: Although 14 per cent alcohol, there is still perceptible residual sugar in the wine! It is full of tropical fruit, especially banana and pineapple.

EVALUATION
: This is 100 per cent Chenin Blanc, and the winemaker attempted to go for a Sauternes, late-ripening impression with this wine. A trace of the attempt has made it into the wine itself. Nevertheless, the wine is out of balance. Thus, I rate it as GOOD. The price is its greatest virtue—a mere Rs. 326.

✠ SAUVIGNON BLANC (12.5%) 2004

EYE: Pale gold with ever-so-slight, but attractive bubbles.

NOSE: Strange hints of barley, almost smelling of beer.

TASTE: Dry and acidic, with crisp, fresh citrus/lemon acids.

EVALUATION

There is Chenin Blanc in the blend, though it is primarily Sauvignon. Although the acid is overpowering, the freshness is the best feature. At Rs. 397, the wine is AVERAGE.

✠✠✠✠ ZINFANDEL (12.5%) 2004

EYE: Cloudy, light-to-medium red (unfiltered and thus cloudy, should be bright and clear at the time of bottling).

NOSE: Very young and fresh fruit-like, with injections of rose and raspberry.

TASTE: Nice coating of tannin (though not far back in the mouth) mixed with strange yeast predominance (will mellow with filtration), a bit of disconnected alcohol, and mixed with the intense clove, one gets a numbing sensation on the palate.

EVALUATION

Impressive wine showing potential; I think there is a great future for Indian Zinfandel! At present, however, work needs to be done in the direction of balance and elegance. Still the wine is VERY GOOD, especially at Rs. 353.

✠✠✠✠ CABERNET SHIRAZ (12.5%) 2004

EYE: Rich, dark garnet with purple flashes.

NOSE: Intense stem and spice, with bursts of capsicum. Delicious chocolate toast (medium-burn oak chips have been added to the fermentation tanks).

TASTE: Heavy toast, full, tannic, a real mouthful for once!

EVALUATION

I was so impressed with the full body of the wine that I was alarmed that such a wine would have no market in India. However, this is the future of quality Indian wines, and this blend itself is certainly VERY GOOD. The price is Rs. 369.

CONCLUSION

Flamingo is a winery to watch. When their wines are regularly available on the market, I will be eagerly sampling each new vintage and experiment they try out. There are hazards they need to avoid, however. One is the all-too-common practice of overdosing with sulphur dioxide. Nevkar says he tries to keep the dose down at 30 parts per million (ppm), but I have trouble believing this. Another problem is endemic with the new producers: bad English, bad labels, bad descriptions of the wines, and so on. Flamingo has a potentially outstanding product, but they need to make sure they do not mess everything up with poor marketing and poorer label design. I hope their reasonable pricing sets a trend.

GRENO VINEYARDS

(Greengold Wine)
Gat 659, Post Bedag,
Tal – Miraj, Dist. Sangli, 416 410.

Greno is starting small, although they have the capacity to produce 100,000 litres of wine. They are off to a good start, however, with two premium wines, both white, on the market:

1. Chenin Blanc
2. Sauvignon Blanc

Both these wines are from Greno's 2004 crushing. They crushed small amounts of red—a Cabernet Sauvignon and a Shiraz—in 2005, but they have not brought these out onto the market yet. They also plan to bring out a post-production blend Rosé, but first they are testing the waters with their two whites.

✦✦✦✦ CHENIN BLANC (12.5%) 2004

EYE: A very luscious, green gold, with fantastically rich legs.

NOSE: Grapy, syrupy, no hint at all of alcohol. There is a touch of green, maybe herb. It is slightly corky, which, because of the honey, makes the nose resemble Tokaj (a wine region in Hungary), with the whiff of residual sweetness.

TASTE: It has got decent body and decent balance, nice and buttery. It is a bit sour (guava) with some cinnamon and spice (clove). I love the green-apple finish.

EVALUATION

This is 100 per cent Chenin Blanc, and it stands out from among others on the market. I rate it as GOOD. The price, Rs. 396, being a tad stiff prevents the wine from roping in a VERY GOOD rating.

+++ SAUVIGNON BLANC (13.5%) 2004

EYE: Nice light bronze, medium rich with very fat legs.

NOSE: Mineraly, touch of mildew, and as usual in Indian Sauvignon Blanc, barley beer.

TASTE: Pretty crisp, some of the typical paprika, a touch astringent. The label mentions that the wine displays flavours of gooseberry, but I cannot detect it.

EVALUATION

It is nice, but I feel it is a bit costly at Rs. 400. Thus, I rate it as GOOD.

CONCLUSION

Greno is a high-tech winery with equipment brought in from Italy. They have the experience of growing fruit, as Green Gold has been in the table grape industry for 25 years. They also have the will to produce high-quality products. Thus, they have all the ingredients to produce a good-quality wine. The problem is, I am not sure if they have anything very special or unique to guide them safely through the rough waters created by the stormy competition. We shall watch closely and wish them well.

GROVER VINEYARDS

Ragunathpura, Dodbalapur Taluk
Bangalore District

Grover vineyards is situated in Dodbalapur, in the Nandi Hills. It is one of the oldest domestic wine producers in India, and up until the twenty-first century, Indian wine was pretty much limited to Grover or Indage, or to the products that pass for wine by Shaw Wallace or Bosca and the like.

Grover does not generally make very good wines, but they do price them better than most of the competition. However, their wines are not bad either. They are beginning to improve, the 2004s far superior to anything that came before. They have seven wines currently on the market:

1. Demi-sec Rosé
2. Blanc de Blancs
3. Shiraz Rosé
4. La Reserve Red Wine
5. Cabernet-Shiraz
6. Sauvignon Blanc
7. Viognier-Clairette

✢   DEMI-SEC ROSÉ (12%) 2000

EYE/NOSE/TASTE/EVALUATION: The bottle is corked, and even if it was not, there is no reason for anyone to drink a rosé from 2000, that is, a four-year-old rosé! It is Rs. 330 down the drain. I believe that Grover no longer produces this wine, which is for the best.

✢✢   BLANC DE BLANCS (12%) 2003

EYE: Light intensity gold.
NOSE: Sulphur too pronounced and persistent; some melon.
TASTE: Salt and mineral, dry, decent acids.

EVALUATION

The Blanc de Blancs is made from a minor white grape called Clairette. This is a bit confusing, since 'claret' is the English word for a Bordeaux red wine. Anyway, *blanc* being French for white, *blanc de blancs* is a term used to describe a white wine that is made exclusively from white grapes, as opposed to the very common procedure of making white wine with black grapes. As already explained in Part One, the juice is not left in contact with the grape skins long enough for it to be tainted by the reddish pigments, so white wine remains white, even when made from black grapes. Anyway, the term *blanc de blancs* is rarely used unless to describe sparkling wine or Champagne, but Grover uses it for their white wine. The wine is priced at Rs. 360, and I would judge it as AVERAGE.

✛ ROSÉ (SHIRAZ) 2003

EYE: The robe is reminiscent of the cocktail Tequila sunrise; it is a pinkish onion skin hue, and is very, very thin looking.

NOSE: Pungent with sulphur and sour. Somewhat making up for these deep flaws is a hint of indigenous fruit, such as guava.

TASTE: It is as thin and sour in the mouth as one would predict from the nose. It is sour but not acid; that is, it is flabby, with no structure given by the acid. Its only virtue is the dryness.

FINISH: This is the best part: the finish is packed with all the fruit, present at the front of the mouth.

EVALUATION

It makes a decent base for sangria, or wine supplemented by chopped fresh fruits, with some soda and maybe sherry. By itself, the rosé makes for difficult drinking. However, I believe that when you can get a very fresh bottle, well chilled, it must be better than those I have hitherto had the chance to taste. I have tasted the 2003 (12 per cent alcohol): it is non-vintage, so there should be some regularity each year, unfortunately. I am greatly disappointed by this. It is reasonably priced (for Indian wines) at Rs. 360, a good Rs. 100 less than Sula. But it is not drinkable. POOR.

✦✦✦ LA RESERVE (12%) 2004

This is one of India's classic wines. It has been around for a long time, and has also been considered one of the best for as long as it has been around. It is a blend of Cabernet Sauvignon and Shiraz, and some Indian wine aficionados suggest that it is best drunk chilled. I tasted it at about 18°C, in conformity with the suggestion on the back label which also says: 'Aged in French oak barrel, it has a luscious bouquet of fruit and spices with a distinctive oaken flavour.'

EYE: This is not the most attractive robe imaginable; a strange, watery purple garnet, but at the same time, it does not look deadly. The disc is clear of debris, and the wine looks young and filtered.

NOSE: Again, not terribly attractive, with a pungency that makes one stand at attention. Nevertheless, finally we have an Indian wine that clearly displays varietal characteristics—somewhere in the chaotic aroma there is the Cabernet grape demanding notice. Also, there are hints of tomato ketchup, quite a common feature in the aroma of wines from the hot Rhône valley of France, where Syrah is used.

TASTE: Sharp, foremost, and aridly drying in the mouth. The aroma of ketchup translates directly into taste. There is also a cheesy (sharp Cheddar) finish, which I must say is rather tasty.

EVALUATION

The taste of French oak cannot be detected, but that is not necessarily important. The barrels could be well seasoned and not imparting any of their characteristics. The wine costs Rs. 440, and that puts the price on a par with Sula's Chilean Satori Merlot. The qualities are also basically on a par. Thus, I would give this a GOOD rating.

✦✦✦✦ CABERNET-SHIRAZ (12%) 2004

EYE: Nice, bright and clear, light and more purple than red. Thick, slow-forming legs.

NOSE: Soft oak and good varietal cabernet. A bit closed, inky, not much fruit, mostly tertiary aromas. Still, very clean and thus most attractive. Perhaps a touch of dark red fruit (plum or prune) begins to develop. After 15 minutes of breathing, one detects very clearly something most remarkable: *gulab jamun!*

TASTE: Thin, dry and at first clean, though the finish is sour and rather chemical and unpleasant. However, there does seem to be decent balance in this wine, though leaning a bit toward alcohol.

EVALUATION

Old wine in a new bottle? I think this is simply La Reserve revamped, a new, far better label designed in the new-world style rather than in poor imitation of French practice. Nevertheless, compared to the 2002 La Reserve, this is a far superior wine. Not only that, I paid Rs. 440 for La Reserve whereas the Cabernet-Shiraz was only Rs. 360. At this price, the Cabernet-Shiraz is VERY GOOD.

✛✛ SAUVIGNON BLANC (12%) 2003

EYE: Beautiful deep gold, the most intensely coloured Sauvignon Blanc on the Indian market.

NOSE: Wonderful flint, alive, but then drowned out by sickly sour, vegetative, sulphur.

TASTE: Vegetative and sour, but at least crisp with nice acidity.

EVALUATION

It is AVERAGE, but expensive at Rs. 400.

✛✛✛ VIOGNIER-CLAIRETTE (12%) 2004

EYE: Light gold of medium intensity.

NOSE: Very fragrant, with vanilla cream, Chardonnay-like butter, some pear-drop and steel.

TASTE: Fullish in the mouth, with decent acids, but nevertheless flabby, and a sour finish.

EVALUATION

The main problem with this wine is the sour finish, but almost on the basis of the nose itself it slides into the GOOD category. The price (Rs. 360) helps. The wine is far better with food than alone.

CONCLUSION

Grover is seriously under performing. Their best wines are their new ones, the 2004 Cabernet-Shiraz and the 2004 Viognier-Clairette. La Reserve is passable considering the competition. The other wines are not good. I hope that the newer wines being better is an indication that Grover is working on improving the whole lot. If they work to improve the Grover line while at the same time keeping their better-than-average prices, then I very much look forward to the coming vintages.

INDAGE

(Champagne Indage)
A/p Narayangaon,
Tal. Junner, Dist. Pune, M.S.

What is now called Chateau Indage of the Indage Group has had several names and incarnations since it first got into viticulture back in 1982. This was for many years India's finest domestic producer, although, ironically, it was originally an exclusively export-oriented company. Indage has produced eight labels exclusively for export:

1. Anarkali Red
2. Chhabri White
3. Omar Khayyam BRUT
4. Soma Red
5. Soma White
6. Tantra—Arkavati
7. Tantra—Baramati (red)
8. Tantra—Baramati (blush)

As I have lived abroad for many years, I have seen the reception of Indage wines in Europe and the USA which is basically this: 'Wine from India? Is it possible?' But at least one of these exports is not too bad; it is the jewel among them, Omar Khayyam, India's most well-known (sparkling) wine.

In India, it is sold under a different name: Marquise de Pompadour. It is the same wine, although the false distinction commonly made is that Marquise is cellar aged for only two years, while the exported Khayyam is aged for three years. The truth is that they are both exactly the same wine, and neither is cellar aged for as long as two years.

On the other hand, the export label Soma is one of the most disgusting liquids I have ever had the displeasure of tasting. Soma

Red is a blend of Cabernet with a local grape variety, whereas Soma White is a blend of two finished domestic wines, Chantilli (Chardonnay) and Riviera (Thompson). Strangely, the ingredient wines of Soma sell in India for Rs. 295 and Rs. 385, or an average of Rs. 340, while Soma sells in rich countries like Germany and the USA for only Rs. 250! I cannot recall having tasted Soma White— either I never have, or I have blocked the trauma. I have heard horror stories about Anarkali and Tantra wines.

Thankfully, most of the these labels have by now been discontinued. This move should help to increase the status of Indian wines abroad, or at least repair the damage done by the mostly disgusting wines we are sending out all too often. Now Indage's export-only line includes the Soma wines and a label called Mist of Sahyadri, with a Red made from Cabernet and a White from Chardonnay.

Before we get into the wines themselves, let us learn a few more things about Indage, because it is an interesting company. The company, as mentioned, started in the early 1980s. Before that time, winemaking in India was more or less restricted to sacramental wine, and the surplus products in Goa. These were not good wines back then, and are still not really drinkable today. In the middle of this dearth of wine production, Indage produced Omar Khayyam, and in 1987 the sparkling wine won a Bronze medal at the International Wine and Spirit Competition—a major coup!

Thus, there is no question that India is capable of producing fine wines. This has already been proven by Indage. The question is: Will it make finer wines? Will the companies experience the educated demand required to energize them enough to go for more international medals? We all hope so.

To date, Indage has been trying to make money more than to make wine. Only with the introduction of the excellently-marketed Sula brand was there any competition for Indage. This gave Indage a bit of a kick, and they began to work on their product. Also important, the son of the founder (Sham Chougale) returned to India a couple of years back and took a keen interest in wine production. Finally, Indage has hired an energetic, experimental young winemaker, F. Schermesser, who, I must admit, has managed to produce a couple of the best wines that India has ever known. These gems, however, are not for sale.

Still, they show the potential of Indian wines. I will briefly mention these very special wines before going through the list of Indage's line.

The 2004 harvest occurred in mid-January. The usual varieties were collected from the usual vineyards, but this year, the new winemaker had total autonomy and was able to separate certain extraordinary berries from the rest of the piles. These were two whites and two reds, Sauvignon Blanc and Chenin Blanc, Cabernet and Merlot.

Schermesser's own preference is for dry wines with balance; he goes for elegant, easy-to-drink wines rather than the old-fashioned approach of most areas of his native France. The luscious, rich Cabernet that he has created, bursting with fruit and vanillin, is very likely the finest wine ever produced in India. The Merlot, round and soft, is a masterpiece, a paradigm of balance and elegance for Indian wines. The Sauvignon Blanc limited edition, as it were, left long on its lees (sediments settling during fermentation), is beautiful and so is the Chenin Blanc.

These wines that Schermesser made with no concern for sales, the market, or for the fact that the rest of the world thinks that India cannot possibly make great wines, are actually India's greatest wines, but I doubt that they will ever be sold as they have been produced in such small quantities, so they will simply be given as gifts or submitted for competitions abroad. It is inconsequential. What matters is that such wines have been made in India, and it has thereby been shown that India can produce very, very fine wines.

Here is a list of all the domestic wines by Indage currently available on the market:

First what Indage calls its line of vin mousseaux (copying French practice), which is to say sparkling wine:

1.   Joie, cuvee close non-vintage
2.   Marquis de Pompadour, Brut
3.   Chateau Indage Ivy Brut

Next, Indage has a series of what they call varietal vintage wines, which means that these wines are made mostly from one specific grape varietal (for example, Chardonnay), or in some cases two specific varietals, and also that each new harvest produces a new wine. That is, wine from 2003 is the 2003 vintage, and wine from 2004 is the 2004 vintage and so on. Non-vintage wine, which Indage also has, may be from grapes harvested in any year, and mixed carefully in order to try to produce a consistent taste for a particular label like Chantilli (discussed below). Thus, Chantilli wine does not have a year on the label, because it might be a mix of grapes harvested in 2001 and 2002 for example—so it is a non-vintage wine.

But back to the line of varietal vintage wines. Indage calls these wines Ivy. New crushes in 2003 (bottled/labelled in 2004) were:

4.   IVY Viognier
5.   IVY Semillon/Chardonnay
6.   IVY Shiraz

And from 2002 (labelled 2003), there was an interesting range:

7. IVY Sauvignon/Semillon
8. IVY White Zinfandel
9. IVY Malbec
10. IVY Chenin/Muscat

Now to the varietal non-vintage that have been around for a long time. They are very basic, neither very good, nor very bad, but certainly Indian classics. With new marketing tactics and fancy labels, these wines are now also being sold as vintage wines:

11. Chantilli Chardonnay
12. Chantilli Cabernet Sauvignon
13. Riviera Red Wine
14. Riviera White Wine

The last category in the domestic produce of Indage is what they call the vin nouveau. In the West, this French term is used to signify wine that is quickly fermented and vinified and ready to drink soon after the harvest. The most famous vin nouveau in the world is Beaujolais nouveau. Such wine is generally meant to be drunk chilled, within six months of bottling.

However, it is not clear if this world-wide definition is the one Indage is employing, considering that there are two Ports on the list. It seems Indage is simply trying to give a fancy foreign name to what is actually a very bad series of wines. These include:

15. Figuera Ruby Port
16. Vin Ballet Red Wine
17. Figuera Tawny Port
18. Vin Ballet White Wine

The Ports, being fortified wines, are beyond the scope of this book. Thus, we have a total of 16 domestically produced Indage wines to taste and evaluate. (There are also joint-venture wines; that is, wine imported by Indage in bulk, labelled/bottled and distributed in India by Indage. These, being imported wines, are covered in Part Three.)

⊹⊹   JOIE, CUVEE CLOSE (12.5%) NON-VINTAGE

EYE: Dull golden biscuit, big, unattractive bubbles.
NOSE: Some mineral (nickel) aromas, but basically flat.
TASTE: Flat and uninspired, no fruit.

EVALUATION

This is a blend of Grenache and Ugni Blanc. There is nothing repulsive nor attractive about it except the price which is Rs. 370. By Indian standards it is cheap bubbly (though certainly not by international standards), so perhaps it is fine to serve at brunches, topped up with orange juice. AVERAGE.

+++ MARQUISE DE POMPADOUR, BRUT (12.5%) 2004

EYE: Bright gold with good stream of not-too-fine bubbles.
NOSE: Mouth-watering fresh bread (yeasty) and white flowers.
TASTE: Crisp and clean, fruity and round. Somewhat cloying.

EVALUATION

Overall the wine is good, though there are some discrepancies—I do not understand the way the Pinot shows up in it, is it from a syrup? This is supposed to be a blend of Pinot Noir, Ugni Blanc, and Chardonnay, though it is perhaps Pinot Meunier, and Chardonnay, with some strange defrosted Pinot Noir syrup added. I cannot say for sure. The other problem is with the fizz— some bottles are highly problematic. I was told at the factory that the inner sides of the Indian-made bottles were not sufficiently smooth and thus the riddling process went wrong in many cases. These bottles have been exchanged with imported bottles, so the problem should be solved. Nevertheless, I must admit that I have trouble pronouncing the wine as GOOD because of the Rs. 600 price tag.

++ CHATEAU INDAGE IVY BRUT (12.5%) 2004

EYE: Bright clear straw robe, decent fizziness.
NOSE: Some tree fruit (apples) with some peach hints developing after a bit. Nice.
TASTE: Disappointing after the nose, it is a flat, toned-down wine, short on acid and body.

EVALUATION

This is supposed to be a 'smooth' bubbly for local (that is, Indian) tastes, but I object to the principle that the Indian market is not ready for high quality, full-flavoured wines. This Brut is vintage, and brings a different blend every year. In 2002 there was Chardonnay, Riesling, and Muscat, whereas the 2004 was Chardonnay, Chenin Blanc, Riesling, and Muscat. Rs. 550 is far too much to ask for this lacklustre wine. AVERAGE.

❖❖❖ IVY VIOGNIER (12.5%) 2004

EYE: Medium gold with lemon-yellow edge.

NOSE: Closed somewhat from sulphur, nickel, banana cream pudding.

TASTE: Soft, medium rich, good soft acids, with some cream. Finish gets chalky and almost sour, with a touch of clove.

EVALUATION

It is interesting how similar this Ivy is to Grover's Viognier. Seems that Indian Viogniers have similar properties beyond the berry itself (since neither Viognier is similar to French Viogniers). While the Ivy is a better wine, the Grover is a better buy, being over Rs. 100 cheaper. The Ivy is Rs. 460, and GOOD.

❖❖❖ IVY SEMILLON/CHARDONNAY (12.5%) 2004

EYE: Light to medium gold, somewhat pale.

NOSE: Wet wood or cork, damp, cashew nuts, thankfully low sulphur.

TASTE: Very creamy, slightly grapy, short on acid. Dry and pretty tasty finish, with a hint of white raisins.

EVALUATION

The wine is expensive at Rs. 460, but it is GOOD. In fact, in terms of form, this might be India's best white wine. It is well structured, pretty elegant, and there is nothing in the least off-putting about it (nothing sour, acrid, astringent, no sulphur, etc.). The problem, in terms of content, is that it is completely unexciting.

+++++ IVY SHIRAZ (12.5%) 2003

EYE: Dark red of medium intensity with purple edges. Nice legs.

NOSE: Light burn oak, very pleasant, and very gamey and appetizing like Gigondas (a French wine from the Rhône which uses Syrah or Shiraz). Smokey, steely, flinty and a lot of camphor wax.

TASTE: Pretty nicely balanced, integrated tannin, though leaning toward alcohol. Very warm and rich. Good finish, only flaw is the acid, which is more sour than fresh.

EVALUATION

Not elegant, but very Rhône, this must currently be India's best red wine. EXCELLENT especially for Rs. 460.

++ IVY SAUVIGNON/SEMILLON (12%) 2003

EYE: Pale straw, some greenish shine.

NOSE: Fresh bread (slightly yeasty), very clean and somewhat floral.

TASTE: Very heady and way out of balance, bitter finish.

EVALUATION

Rather disappointing for the price (Rs. 460). AVERAGE.

++ IVY WHITE ZINFANDEL (12%) 2003

EYE: This is a very thin, but bright wine, with a salmon to tangerine-coloured robe.

NOSE: Only sulphur, and then some fish, perhaps, the same salmon gave it its colour? After some 30 minutes of breathing, a hint of peach is detectible.

TASTE: At first it tastes simply of grape syrup with alcohol added, but after one gets used to it, it makes for pleasant drinking—resiny, with a taste of white raisins, and decent enough, considering that it is dry.

EVALUATION

AVERAGE, and a bit costly at Rs. 450. The 2004 is better, though it also seems unclean and unrounded with sharp, searing acid.

++++ IVY MALBEC (12%) 2004

EYE: Light red with disturbingly watery edge.
NOSE: Very heady, the alcohol must actually be more than 13 per cent. Oak is detectible.
TASTE: Nice and firm, warm, a bit closed due to alcohol predominance, but pretty tasty overall.

EVALUATION

Malbec is a grape variety used in Bordeaux blends to provide colour and tannin. I do not recall seeing it used alone as a varietal wine, although it might happen around the Mediterranean. Nevertheless, it seems to work. The wine is somewhat costly at Rs. 425, but I would still say that it is VERY GOOD.

+ IVY CHENIN/MUSCAT (12%) 2004

EYE: Light gold, very low intensity.
NOSE: Closed (full of sulphur dioxide).
TASTE: Literally tastes of rubbish, very sour.

EVALUATION

Perhaps this is a problem with the individual bottle, but I am guessing it is actually the wine—at Rs. 460, this is no better than POOR.

++ CHANTILLI CHARDONNAY (12.5%) 2004

EYE: Medium gold.
NOSE: Buttery, which is indicative of the presence of Chardonnay. Also a touch of oak.
TASTE: Pretty decent mouthful, perhaps, there is really a good percentage of Chardonnay in the wine which is good.

EVALUATION

The wine is AVERAGE, but hard to recommend at Rs. 385.

CHANTILLI CABERNET
SAUVIGNON (12%) 2004 & 2005

EYE: Thinnish, medium red robe with purple hue.

NOSE: Almost exclusively wood, touch of dough and then cherry pits and watermelon after opening up. No complexity, but warm and pleasant enough.

TASTE: Decent tannin coating, though not far back. Some candy taste, but the finish is astringent.

EVALUATION

AVERAGE, but costly at Rs. 385.

The 2005 (12.5%) is better than the 2004.

EYE: It is still too thin and the disc is not clear.

NOSE: The nose is suggestive of more Cab-Sav, with a characteristic whiff of fatty ham.

TASTE: The taste is disappointing due to a very chemical, biting element. It is tannic and dry. At Rs. 390 it is still AVERAGE.

RIVIERA RED WINE (12.5%) 2003

EYE: Very light red and rather watery.

NOSE: Nothing like Pinot, but hard to detect much more than sulphur.

TASTE: Without structure, splashes about like a juice, no hint of Pinot. Some unripe red fruit.

EVALUATION

The label on the bottle states: 'Riviera Red Wine is made from Pinot Noir.' This cannot be true. It goes on to say it is 'a light, dry, wine', which is true. It also says: 'it's refreshing and fruity', which is not really true. It also adds that the wine has 'an excellent strawberry bouquet' which is not true. The wine is not too bad. I wonder what the grape is, though, because it is obviously not Pinot. AVERAGE, but not worth Rs. 300.

RIVIERA WHITE WINE (12.5%) 2003 & 2004

EYE: The disc is clear, no floaters. The robe is a dark lemon yellow, quite intensely yellow, in fact, but at the same time the wine is watery, not viscous—a bit strange. Legs are normal.

NOSE: Whereas Chardonnay tends to have certain identifiable characteristics (see Part One), I am unable to distinguish the peculiar Chardonnay aromas here. Ugni Blanc is also a difficult one to detect, basically, what I get above all else is surely a pungent whiff of yeast. There are also some distinct hints of pork, as well as citrus.

TASTE: Acid is dominant, almost searing. The overall feel is sticky but surprisingly not watery, rather luscious in fact. I feel that the acid is so disjointed from the wine structure that some sort of acidification must have taken place. Acid may have been poured into the must after fermentation. There is a hint of cheddar cheese, which may be the only showing of the Chardonnay grape. The finish is sour and unpleasant.

EVALUATION

This was the 2003 Riviera, a blend of Ugni Blanc and Chardonnay. According to Indage, 'it has a fresh, fruity taste, and a hint of exotic limes with floral, grassy bouquet.' I am afraid this is a direct quotation off the label, so the bad grammar has been institutionalized, as it were. The 2004 is better, with the acid more integrated and a good whiff of peach developing after the yeast dies down. Rs. 320 is simply too much to ask for this wine. AVERAGE.

✛ VIN BALLET RED WINE (12.5%) 2003 & 2004

EYE: Light red with purple edges.

NOSE: Jammy, grapy, undeveloped and not too attractive.

TASTE: Same as the nose, but less acceptable.

EVALUATION

They say this has Gamay, the grape used in Beaujolais, and perhaps this is what led Indage to refer to this as a Nouveau wine. It is blended with Arkeshyam, allegedly, and the overall result is pretty bad, whatever the price. POOR.

⊹⊹ VIN BALLET WHITE WINE (12.5%) 2003 & 2004

This is a blend of Ugni blanc, reportedly with the native grape Arkavati, though I think it is actually Thompson. I have tasted one bottled in 2003; in other words, I tasted a bottle of 'vin nouveau' a year after the harvest, which is generally ill advised.

EYE: Bright yellow gold.
NOSE: Pleasant and fresh with hints of melon and pear.
TASTE: Dry and sulphuric with an interesting dose of banana. The balance leans heavily to acid—it is watery and acidic.

EVALUATION

As stated, I tasted this at least six months after one should; on the other hand, it is hardly available at the right time in wine stores in India, so it is probable that most people will get hold of the bottle too late. The wine is AVERAGE, the fresher and colder the better. The 2004 is no better than the 2003. The nose is unclean and full of sulphur. The only virtue is the acid, which balances the cloying tendency of the wine.

CONCLUSION

That is the full line of Indage's domestic wines. It is the largest wine producer in India, and captures about 71 per cent of the entire market. This will change slowly as new producers emerge but Indage is itself continuing to develop, so it is going to be able to hold on to its number one position for quite some time to come.

Indage also has a line of very drinkable wines which it refers to as its 'global joint ventures'. What this basically means is that wine from France, Germany, South Africa, Australia, etc., is shipped to India in big bladders, and then bottled and labelled in India. I am very keen about this method of importing, because it serves to avoid some of the bite of the enormously high tariffs placed by the government on imported wines, while at the same time providing some labour within India itself. Such wines—that is, imported in bulk and bottled/labelled in India—will be covered in Part Three, which deals with international wine.

Indage is a strange bird. On the one hand, it makes some of India's best wine today, but on the other hand, it is grossly under performing. Notice that out of 16 wines, only four were good or above. This is a shame. Indage has the means to change this scenario, but it is not clear whether they have the will.

N.C. FINE WINES

(Fouray)
A/p. Nerlie, Tal. Kadegaon,
Dist. Sangli

N.C. Fine Wines is a small winery in Maharashtra, with 25,000 litre capacity and producing only one wine, a red called Fouray.

✢ FOURAY RED WINE (12.5%) 2003

EYE/NOSE/TASTE/EVALUATION: The bottle I procured was either completely off, or the wine itself is totally undrinkable. Let me be charitable and assume that only this bottle was corked, and this does not reflect upon the wine itself. Nevertheless, I am suspicious. It sells for Rs. 175, and is made from Isabella grapes.

N.D. WINES

Pimpalgaon, Wani Road,
At Po. Khedgaon, Tal. Dindori,
Dist. Nashik, 422205, M.S.

N.D. Wines is one of the new, upcoming players on the Indian wine scene. Owned by Mr. Gaikwad, one of the founders of the now defunct Sparkling wine manufacturers, Pimpane, N.D. Wines has constructed a high-tech, modern winery and employed a French Wine Master, Jean-Manual Jacquinot, as their consultant. N.D. Wines is now making some of India's finest wines. The problem is, poor marketing. They were sitting on 150,000 litres of good-quality wine, but had no means of marketing/distributing it. Consequently, they were forced to sell their wine in bulk to Sula, which has somewhat immorally, though not quite illegally, bottled it as its own product.

So, N.D. Wines' 2003 vintage is what you find on sale in wine stores. If you want to try N.D. Wines' 2004 vintage, then buy a bottle of Sula! It is not yet clear whether N.D. will be pulling all the wines under its own labels off the shelf. However, from 2004 onwards, N.D. is now basically just a production facility for Sula. Nevertheless, we shall include and discuss them here, as some of their wines are already available on the retail shelves.

One accomplishment in terms of packaging that N.D. Wines has achieved is that they have bottled every one of their wines in half-bottles (375 ml). This is a great idea for the Indian market, as in many families there is only one drinker, and he or she is not able to finish a full bottle (750 ml) alone before the wine turns sour. The half-bottles are perfect for the people who enjoy one glass of wine a day. Each of the half-bottles of N.D. Wines cost approximately 55 per cent of the price of a whole bottle. For example, a whole bottle of N.D. Chenin Blanc costs Rs. 378; the half bottle costs Rs. 210.

N.D. has eight labels on sale now:

1. N.D. Sauvignon Blanc
2. N.D. Cabernet Sauvignon
3. N.D. Chenin Blanc
4. N.D. Syrah
5. N.D. Cabernet-Syrah
6. N.D. Spaga (Sauvignon Blanc)
7. N.D. Spaga (Cabernet Sauvignon)
8. Hoor

The first five are varietal wines, and N.D. claims that they are 100 per cent of the variety indicated. The Spaga label was for a while called 'Reserve', but then later it was changed to 'Spaga'—this brand is a vineyard-select wine, containing Cabernet or Sauvignon Blanc only from one selected vineyard. In European practice (remember, their winemaker is French), this generally results in a better, more concentrated wine, since the vineyard selected would be one of the best sites available. In Europe, this distinction is indicated by actually naming the vineyard on the label. In the New World instead, a term like 'Estate' would be used, but then generally the vineyard is on the winery estate unlike N.D.'s vineyards. 'Reserve', on the other hand, generally refers to special ageing of the wine, and not to the location of the vineyard. Thus, because of these various problems, N.D. could not think of how to label their one-vineyard selected Cabernet and Sauvignon Blanc. They made the unfortunate decision of calling them *Spaga*.

Besides the bad-sounding name 'Spaga', the labels too that N.D. have chosen are sub-standard. Ideally, none of this should matter if the quality of the wine were high. However, packaging and marketing do matter a great deal. N.D. Wines had made the grave error of focussing only on production, and they have left their packaging and labelling to less capable hands. (This, by the way, is the polar opposite of a company like Sula, which has put all its money and resources into packaging, labelling, and marketing, and precious little into quality.)

But as a result of these fatal errors, N.D. Wines, as a brand, essentially, no longer exists. This is a great shame, because as I have already said, N.D. made some of India's best wines.

✦✦ N.D. SAUVIGNON BLANC (13.5%) 2003

EYE: Straw or light gold, somewhat watery.
NOSE: Not very clean, some mineral, a lot of alcohol.
TASTE: Very heady, very acid, not terribly well balanced.

EVALUATION

The wine is decent, but not worth Rs. 408. On the whole, I would say it is AVERAGE.

✦✦✦ N.D. CABERNET SAUVIGNON (13.5%) 2003

EYE: Intense red, but nevertheless rather watery edges.
NOSE: Pronounced cheddar cheese, burnt rubber, yeast and capsicum.
TASTE: Thin, a decent tannin coating, some berry character, but very chemical, sulphur dioxide. Also somewhat green. Very similar to the Spaga (see below), but less mellow, and more acrid.

EVALUATION

The wine gets much better after a good 20 minutes of breathing. The main problem with the wine is that there must have been some trouble with mercaptans during fermentation, and the brew was treated with too much sulphur. It is just too chemical, but again, with breathing this tones down. I like this wine more than the Spaga, although it is easy to see that if the Spaga had no trouble during fermentation, then it would have been a more elegant wine. I would suggest anyone to buy the Cabernet Sauvignon over the Spaga, since it is a much better buy at Rs. 360. The wine is GOOD.

✦✦ N.D. CHENIN BLANC (13.5%) 2003

EYE: Pale lemon yellow.
NOSE: Mostly sour, pickling vinegar, unattractive.
TASTE: Predominantly yeast and acid, thin and dry. The only nice thing is the cheesy flavour, but otherwise very lame.

EVALUATION

At Rs. 378, it is a bad buy. The wine is AVERAGE.

⊹⊹ N.D. SYRAH (13.5%) 2003

EYE: Rich garnet, attractive. Slight sparkle, petillance.

NOSE: A lot of sulphur at first, but it then opens up to a floral bouquet.

TASTE: Intense mineral, salt and spice. Sweaty sock, indicative of Syrah. But some rather off, numbing taste.

EVALUATION

This has the potential to be a very good wine. The sparkle indicates that the wine was not properly stabilized, and there may have been some malolactic fermentation occurring in the bottle. That could account for the off taste. At Rs. 540, I feel cheated. I hope other bottles are free of the problem my bottle had. The wine is AVERAGE.

⊹⊹⊹ N.D. CABERNET-SYRAH (13.5%) 2003

EYE: Darkest, most intense robe that I have seen on an Indian wine. A ring of bubbles/film along the edge, suggesting instability in the wine.

NOSE: Lovely red liquorice, warm, some stone of plum.

TASTE: Jammy, mild tannin coat, pretty decent balance. Burst of caramel. Finish of tobacco. The tobacco is delicious, reminiscent of South African Shiraz.

EVALUATION

The wine is pretty good, just that it is thin and tending toward sour. I would recommend it without hesitation had it not been priced as high as Rs. 492. It is not a good buy, though it is GOOD.

⊹⊹/⊹⊹⊹ N.D. SPAGA (SAUVIGNON BLANC) (13.5%) 2003

EYE: Pale gold of light-medium intensity.

NOSE: Sweet-and-sour, pineapple, almost like a Chinese dish! Intense Hungarian spicy paprika.

TASTE: Rather elegant, nice and dry, but the acids are too harsh.

EVALUATION

It is only AVERAGE if drunk alone, but with food it is GOOD. However, at Rs. 540, it is impossible to recommend.

⁺⁺ N.D. SPAGA (CABERNET SAUVIGNON) (13.5%) 2003

EYE: Intense red, but nevertheless rather watery edges.

NOSE: Pronounced cheddar cheese, burnt rubber, yeast and capsicum.

TASTE: Thin, a decent tannin coating, some berry character, but very chemical, sulphur dioxide. Also somewhat green.

EVALUATION

As you can see, this wine hardly differs from the non-Spaga Cab-Sav. It gets much better after 20 minutes of breathing. The problem is that there must have been some trouble with mercaptans during fermentation, and the brew was treated with too much sulphur. It is just too chemical, but again, with breathing this tones down. I like the wine. But not worth Rs. 582, though, no matter what. AVERAGE.

⁺⁺/⁺⁺⁺ HOOR (13.5%) 2003

EYE: Beautiful gold of medium intensity.

NOSE: Excellent nose, packed with fresh fruit (apples, apricot, pear) as well as nutmeg. In the beginning there is some pronounced maderization/sherry, but after breathing this gives way to a new load of spice.

TASTE: Heady, oily and slick, dry with a sour, copper finish. Quite a disappointment after the lovely nose.

EVALUATION

I suspect that some indigenous grapes have been tossed into the blend, because the nose is just too aromatic. If the taste matched the nose, this would be an excellent white. As it stands, it would drop down to AVERAGE were it not for the decent price (Rs. 340), which pushes it up to GOOD. By the way, I cannot avoid mentioning that the half-bottle Hoor is of an exceptional value, sold for less than half the price of the full bottle. If the price is not increased of the 375 ml bottle (currently Rs. 142), then the half-size Hoor would be India's best wine value.

CONCLUSION

N.D. Wines make pretty good wine, but very bad labels. The Spaga, which they should have called 'Select', is outrageously priced. On the other hand, they also have a great value wine in the half-bottle Hoor. All in all, N.D. Wines would have been a great addition to the Indian wine scene. Instead, they have become an addition to Sula's production capacity.

PRATHAMESH WINES

Pimpaldar, Tal. Satana,
Dist. Nashik, M.S.

Prathamesh Wines is one of the smaller wineries of Maharashtra, with a capacity of 50,000 litres, and an actual production, in 2004, of 44,000 litres, of which 18,000 litres are Red Wine and 26,000 litres White Wine.

Prathamesh has three labels:

1. Red Wine (Cabernet Sauvignon)
2. White Wine (Chenin Blanc)
3. Rosé Wine

Unfortunately, each of Prathamesh's wines that I examined were corked. This is a perennial problem in India, where the hot and bumpy shipping of potentially good wine jeapordizes it, and then the hot and dirty storage of the wine in shops finishes it off completely. Anyway, each Prathamesh wine sells for Rs. 365, and the Rosé is actually just a blend of the Red and White wines post-production—not a great idea.

PRINCESS

(In-Vogue Creations)
Taloja, M.S.

Princess wines are apparently manufactured by In-Vogue Creations, a winery based in Taloja. I have no information about the winery, although I have tasted the two wines that they produce:

1. Princess White Wine
2. Princess Red Wine

Both labels include very strange text and/or descriptions, which I cannot resist reproducing here. The White Wine label reads: 'In Memory of le Chateâu du Plassis'; what in the world might this mean? It also states that the wine is 'demi-sec', or semi-sweet, and that it is 'a light bodied and mellow wine made from carefully selected Indian grapes in the finest French tradition.' I am not sure what this could mean either.

The Red Wine is described as 'a full-bodied, honest wine, exclusively manufactured from carefully selected, individually hand-picked grapes'. Very strange.

✢ PRINCESS WHITE WINE (13.1%) 2004

EYE: Nearly clear wine, but cloudy. Profuse tears suggestive of high residual sugar.

NOSE: The nose is like that of Vermouth, though dirtier—perhaps the wine has been fortified with grape spirit.

TASTE: It is full and rich with a syrupy sweetness. Though the nose indicates fortification, in the mouth the alcohol is well integrated and mild, reminds one of cheap German wine.

EVALUATION

The crazy label, the screw-top, and the funny bottle would warn any real wine drinker away from Princess. I am rather suspicious of it, though selling at Rs. 120, which is the same price as Bosca, I would recommend Princess over Bosca any day. POOR.

✢ PRINCESS RED WINE (13.1%) 2004

EYE: Filthy watery orange-red; I have never seen anything like it. Looks dangerous.

NOSE: Like cheap vermouth, watered down.

TASTE: Mild, sweet and juicy, basically like a punch. I doubt if it is wine.

EVALUATION

The packaging is as bad as Princess White's, and I am not even sure if this is wine. Rs. 120 is too much. POOR.

PYRAMID WINES

MIDC Area, Plot No. E-200,
Baramati, Dist. Pune, M.S.

Pyramid is a winery with 100,000 litre capacity, but they make only one wine, and this too primarily for export. The wine is called Yellowstone. It is a well-packaged Cabernet Sauvignon-Shiraz blend, and sells for Rs. 190.

Unfortunately, I have not had the chance to taste/evaluate Yellowstone.

RAJDHEER WINES

Bhilwad, Post. Kapsi, Tal. Deola,
Dist. Nashik, 423 120, M.S.

Rajdheer Wines is a small producer that is starting out. They have a capacity of 40,000 litres, and that capacity is fully utilized at present. They are holding 30,000 litres of red wine from their 2003 harvest, and have 10,000 litres of white wine from the 2004 harvest (which was in March 2004).

For the time being, they are producing two wines:

1. Le Vino Red Wine
2. Aurum White Wine

In the long term, Rajdheer plans to produce the following varietal wines: Sauvignon Blanc, Chardonnay, Cabernet Sauvignon, Zinfandel, and Shiraz.

It is only because of these noble plans that Rajdheer is included in the current edition of the Wine Guide. Look out for these wines if and when they hit the market.

✣ AURUM CHENIN BLANC (13%) 2004

EYE: A dull gold, not clear.
NOSE: A shocking smell of formaldehyde
TASTE: A disgusting mix of saliva and stale beer.

EVALUATION

This is an absolute waste of money at Rs. 480. POOR.

✣ LE VINO RED WINE (12.5%) 2004

EYE: The robe looks terribly maderized. It is very cloudy with a nearly clear edge.
NOSE: It stinks of formaldehyde.
TASTE: There is a repulsive tongue-coating film—I had to spit out the wine.

EVALUATION

The wine is very bad, and it is waste of Rs. 340. The label claims oak-ageing, but this is obviously untrue. POOR.

SAIKRIPA WINERY

A-68, Additional MIDC, Palus
Tal. Palus, Dist. Sangli - 416 310, M.S.

Saikripa is a sleepy little winery located on the Palus wine park. It is a small producer that is just trying to get itself off the ground. Most of their wine is not yet bottled, sitting in chilling tanks waiting for the market to coax it out into the world.

For the time being, they are producing only two wines:

1. Syrah
2. Cabernet/Merlot

⧾⧾ SYRAH (FROM THE VAT, UNFILTERED) 2004

EYE: Dark cloudy purple with cherry-coloured streaks.

NOSE: Loads and loads of raspberry and cherry tomatoes—just packed with fruit!

TASTE: Somewhat too sour and thin, but it has good mouth feel.

EVALUATION

At Rs. 250, it is good value. AVERAGE.

⧾⧾⧾ CABERNET/MERLOT (13.5%) 2004

EYE: Wonderfully clear, medium garnet, just a bit thin.

NOSE: Great clean nose, floral, hints of pepper, classic Merlot aroma.

TASTE: Thinnish, but good acids, a pleasant drinking wine—the main flaw is the sour finish.

EVALUATION

I like the wine as a simple, everyday drinking wine. The price is also right, at Rs. 349. GOOD.

SAILO WINES

(V.M. AGROSOFT)
A/p. Pimpalgaon Baswant, Tal. Niphad,
Dist. Nashik, 422 209, M.S.

Sailo Wines is a great success story. Although a small winery, with a capacity of 25,000 litres, Sailo's sales are the third highest in India, behind Indage and Sula—the two major players in the Indian market. The reason for its success? Simplicity.

Sailo has two labels, both reds:

1.   Et Tu Brutus
2.   Mark Antony

Sailo is owned and operated by Vishwas More, whose father has been the behind-the-scenes founder of Indian wines. Whereas Mr. Chougale of Indage, a rich industrialist and businessman, may have been the one to set up the first Indian wine empire, it is actually Mr. More, a simple but clever and hardworking grape farmer who lobbied with the Maharashtra government to support the fledgling wine industry, to open wine parks and wine institutes, and to permit grape farmers to produce their own wines. This eliminated exploitative middlemen who would buy grapes from farmers at subsistence prices and then sell them to wineries at handsome profits.

Even Pimpane, the legendary first Indian sparkling wine factory, was the brainchild of Mr. More. Pimpane failed, partly because the idea was too visionary and before its time. Now the younger More has returned to the wine scene, and at the most opportune time. Sailo (V.M. Agrosoft) was licensed in 2001, and had its first harvest in 2003. The 2003 sold well, and now Vishwas has bottled the 2004.

When visiting the winery, I could not resist asking about the quirky names given to the wines. Vishwas' daughter is named Saili, and her nickname is Sailo, hence the brand name. As for Et Tu Brutus and Mark Antony, it turns out that Vishwas studied at a convent school, where Shakespeare's *Julius Caesar* had been often forced down his throat, as it were.

✦✦   ET TU BRUTUS (12.5%) 2003, MISLABELLED 2002

EYE: A very light red with a lot of purple streaks.
NOSE: Perfumed, mostly raspberries.
TASTE: Thin and without body. Heavy raspberry flavours.

EVALUATION

There is so much raspberry in this that I first thought it was a raspberry wine rather than a wine made from grapes. It is made from Isabella, which makes very light wines. The problem is that it has no depth, body, tannin, or any element that makes a good wine, except the fruit. On the other hand, the wine is selling so well, that I realize that this light, fruity, un-wine is something that appeals to many people's taste (or lack thereof). Anyway, it is pretty cheap at Rs. 185, and AVERAGE.

✦✦   MARK ANTONY (12.5%) 2003,
       MISLABELLED 2002

EYE: Light-to-medium intensity red, very clean and clear.

NOSE: There is a nice whiff of oak in the nose, but also with some burnt rubber indicative of mercaptans.

TASTE: Warm, with decent tannin, but unstructured, grapy, and very foxy.

EVALUATION

There is a big jump in quality between Antony and Brutus. The addition of Cabernet to the Antony helps a lot, but it is still not up to standard. AVERAGE.

However, the Mark Antony 2004, which I have tasted, is again a far superior wine to the 2003. The EYE of the 2004 is already more intense than the 2003, as there was even more Cabernet in the 2004. The NOSE had caramel and cola, probably arising from the Isabella, but the TASTE had a nice Beaujolais Nouveau smack to it, with jammy flavours, neither rich nor balanced, but clean and decent. There is some creamy vanilla which is nice, and the touch of oak will continue to be welcome.

Note that on the back label of Mark Antony, the Pinot grape is mentioned. This is a mistake. Antony is actually a Cabernet Sauvignon, with Isabella added for volume.

CONCLUSION

Vishwas has promised me that the next Mark Antony will be with greater concentration, more Cabernet less Isabella, and possibly even a good deal of Shiraz, as the Mores have recently planted four acres of Shiraz. At Rs. 257, Antony will, in the near future, be a good wine and possibly India's best bargain.

SHAW WALLACE

Gulab Bhawan, 6 Bahadur Shah Zafar Marg,
New Delhi 110 002

Shaw Wallace and Company Limited is one of the major liquor production companies of India, and concentrates far more on its hard spirits than on its 'wine'. I put wine in quotation marks because I am not sure that the beverage that Shaw Wallace sells as wine is actually entitled to the name.

Shaw Wallace claims that it guides its industry 'with a view to keep up with the demands of the consumer. Is this true?

You have probably heard of their wine: Golconda Ruby Wine.

✣   GOLCONDA RUBY WINE (NON-VINTAGE)

Golconda Ruby Wine is one of the oldest Indian wines available on the market, and might single-handedly be responsible for the miserable reputation of domestic Indian wine. It was first produced by Shaw Wallace in 1967 at Hyderabad. After prohibition was declared in Andhra Pradesh (possibly as a result of lawmakers having tasted Golconda), the wine production shifted to Bangalore, where it is currently produced.

Golconda is, I believe, the best selling domestic wine on the Indian market, with an annual sales volume of over 100,000 cases!

This wine is produced from a grape variety known locally as 'Bangalore Blue', grown, as the name implies, around the Bangalore region.

EYE: Light red, watery.
NOSE: Sulphuric and grapy, some disconnected alcohol.
TASTE: Watery, sickly sweet and yet with a terribly sour finish.

EVALUATION

This wine is terrible. According to Shaw Wallace, Golconda 'is crisp with a subtle sweet taste and a robust flavour.' The truth is, there is nothing subtle about the sweetness, and calling the flavour 'robust' is a euphemism of the highest order. POOR.

CONCLUSION

I suppose Shaw Wallace has nothing to lose (for the time being, anyway), by producing such a wine. It is one of the few members of the alcoholic beverages industry in the world which can boast the sale of 11 liquor bottles every second. It is a self-proclaimed 'liquor giant' of the country, and more questionably claims 'to speak the language of change and development in keeping with changing tastes and trends'. Let us hope they mean it, and start producing real wine. Remember, the burden is not only on them, but on us too: consumers have to demand quality products; no company operates on the principle of charity. They will make no better product than demanded, indeed, they will try to make the worst that they can get away with, because that is how profit margins are increased. And for too long we have been letting Indian producers get away with inferior wine.

SULA VINEYARDS

Gat 35/2, Govardhan,
Off Gangapur Road, Dist. Nashik, M.S.

Sula is, in commercial terms, a great success story. In terms of strict winemaking, they leave much to be desired. But the actual quality (or the lack of it) of their wines has not slowed them down in the least: Sula is all about good marketing. Their labels are attractive, their bottles/corks are good, their owner is a media charmer, and they have managed to sell a great deal of their pretty inferior series of wines.

Sula is the darling of domestic Indian wines, or rather of Indian wine, in general, since they not only produce what is popularly regarded as some of India's best wines, but they have also initiated an import regime of great variety, some of very good value.

Sula Vineyards came into being through the strenuous efforts of Mr. Rajeev Samant, who in 1993 began farming on family-owned land in Nashik, at first planting mangoes, and then sometime later grapes for wine production. Despite early stops and starts, since the late 1990s, Sula has been going strong, and I believe it will continue to go strong, provided it can cope with the coming changes in taste, demand, quality, and so on.

Indeed, the origins of Sula are in some way reminiscent of those of Indage, at least in terms of original ambition and zeal. Indage faded, sitting on its laurels and banking on the general apathy of Indian consumers. Sula, being a marketing phenomenon from the very beginning, will likely avoid this path.

Before Samant created Sula, he knew nothing about wine. He was fortunate to have found an optimistic and progressive (shall we say typically Californian?) technical advisor, Kerry Damskey, graduate of one of the world's premier institutes of enology, University of California, Davis. In 1997, Damskey planted the noble European grape variety, Sauvignon Blanc, as well as Chenin Blanc, which had probably never been planted in India before.

Since that time, Sula kept planting and experimenting, and now they have a good range of domestic wines, including sparkling, white, red, and rosé:

Sparkling:
1. Sula Brut
2. Sula Seco

Whites:
3. Sauvignon Blanc
4. Chenin Blanc
5. Madeira White

Reds:
6. Sula Cabernet/Shiraz
7. Madeira Red

Rosés:
8. Blush Zinfandel
9. Madeira Rosé

Additionally, Sula has one white wine (Pacifica Chardonnay) and one red wine (Satori Merlot) which are produced abroad, imported to India, but bottled and labelled in India. These will be covered in Part Three, where imported wines are discussed.

Also, by end 2006, Sula will have introduced two new labels: the so-called Late Harvest Chenin Blanc and Dindori Reserve Shiraz-Cabernet. What do these terms: 'late harvest' and 'reserve' mean in the Indian context?

In traditional winemaking, late harvest means harvesting the grapes later than normal, which means risking damage to the grapes and vines by frost in winter. By delaying the harvest the grapes ripen more and thus the resulting wines are richer and fuller. But in the tropics, the term late harvest cannot mean the same thing, since by harvest time in India, winter is over. Does it, then, refer to harvesting before the monsoon? That makes no sense. Further, the challenge in India is not ripening grapes, as there is enough sunlight here. In India the challenge lies in achieving enough cool hours or enough non-sunlight. Only then there is sufficient acid left to balance the sugars in the ripened berries. Thus, late harvesting in India would give flabby, sickly sweet wines without adequate acidity, which would consequently lead to the nasty practice of acidification or adding acid to the wine to balance the sugars. This may already be a growing problem in India. Creating a late harvest wine will institutionalize this problem.

As for 'reserve', this is a bit more straightforward, and Sula's intentions here are nothing to frown about. They have imported 220 litre capacity, used American and French oak barrels, and the Dindori Reserve is aged in these barrels. Thus, 'reserve' means to be aged in oak, at least for Sula. When other Indian wineries begin using the term 'reserve', we will have to try and figure out what their meaning is as well.

Let us now turn to the present range of Sula wines. We will begin with the sparkling wines.

✠✠✠✠ SULA BRUT (11.5%) 2003

This is a méthode champenoise wine, that is, a sparkling wine which has undergone a secondary fermentation in the very bottle in which it is sold. It is a 'blanc de blancs', made from a blend of three white grape varieties from among eight of Sula's vineyards. The grapes are pneumatically pressed in whole bunches, cold fermented, and then cellared for eighteen months. Though it is non-vintage, the taste changes year to year.

Sula describes their own product as 'a creamy, yet light nectar that goes down like a dream', and suggests that both Sula Seco and Sula Brut be served ice-cold.

I do not disagree with the description of it as 'nectar', but 'creamy' is stretching it. A creamy sparkling wine or Champagne is one where the bubbles tend to be very small and plentiful, thus coating the mouth in a manner reminiscent of cream. The bubbles of Sula Brut, however, are rather on the larger side (for bottle-fermented wines, that is), reminding one more of a vat fermented product.

EYE: The intensity of the hue is somewhat lacking compared to what one likes to see in méthode champenoise wines, and I have already commented on the bubbles.

NOSE: This is a pleasant surprise—no special fruit or aromas, a bit grassy and over metallic, but at least pretty clean and crisp.

TASTE: Nice and dry, refreshing, good presence of biscuity yeast. The finish is a touch sour, but the overall mouth feel is certainly positive.

EVALUATION

For Rs. 550, I would unhesitatingly judge this a VERY GOOD wine.

✠✠ SULA SECO (11.5%) NON-VINTAGE

EYE: Light gold, rather dull, perhaps as a result of ineffective disgorgement.

NOSE: Some nice strawberry, but nothing one looks for in a quality sparkling wine.

TASTE: Tasty peach but very sweet.

EVALUATION

Described as a medium-dry sparkling wine, it is actually cloyingly sweet. Although made by the méthode champenoise, there is no autolytic character, and it could just as well have been vat fermented. The price is pretty good (Rs. 395), but the bubbly is just AVERAGE.

⁜ SAUVIGNON BLANC (13%) 2005

EYE: Light to medium intensity straw.

NOSE: Flinty and fresh, some green grass.

TASTE: Great structure, but far too acid. Dry, refreshing, but sour finish.

EVALUATION

This was India's first Sauvignon Blanc, and in 2002 this was probably India's best wine. The 2003 was variable, while the 2004 was simply disappointing. For Rs. 490 we expect better. AVERAGE.

⁜ CHENIN BLANC (11.5%) 2003

EYE: Light intensity yellow gold.

NOSE: Appetizing, full of fruit.

TASTE: Sickly sweet, all else is masked.

EVALUATION

This was India's first Chenin Blanc. Sula calls it 'semi-dry', but it is actually sickeningly sweet. Outside of India I would give it a POOR rating, but if you can handle the sugar, for Rs. 375 it is AVERAGE.

⁜ CHENIN BLANC (11.5%) 2005

EYE: Light straw of medium intensity.

NOSE: Mellow aroma, pear and white grape.

TASTE: Full and rather sweet, but acids come in after and

stiffen up the wine. However, the balance is off, a seeming disconnect.

EVALUATION

Thankfully the wine is less sweet and far cleaner than before. It has jumped up to GOOD, even at Rs. 440.

++ ## MADERA WHITE WINE NON-VINTAGE (12%) 2004 BATCH TASTED

EYE: Very pale straw, slight sparkle and ring of froth.
NOSE: White grape, somewhat sour, with hint of watermelon rind.
TASTE: A bit slimy, saliva, some lime peel, dull sweet finish.

EVALUATION

Madera is Sula's lower-end product, and the price is attractive (Rs. 205). But just for a lower price, we do not want to compromise entirely on quality. A low quality wine, and not worth Rs. 205. AVERAGE.

++ ## CABERNET/SHIRAZ (13.5%) 2004

EYE: Medium garnet with purple edges.
NOSE: Shiraz character, warm and earthy, with a touch of red fruit and a lot of mineral/steel.
TASTE: Dirty tannin (is it stems?), astringent, with a sour finish. It is so thin and dirty that it seems the skins were repeatedly pressed to get every last drop out of them, or even worse, that the vat was topped up with water to get more volume.

EVALUATION

Sula describes their Cabernet/Shiraz blend by stating that 'ripe cherry and plum fruit with peppery notes mark this smooth, medium-bodied red wine. With nuances of oak, this deep purple wine has great balance and a lingering finish'. This sort of exaggeration is not peculiar to Indian wine companies. Nearly every back label you will find from wines all round the world will be full of this sort of gibberish. Winemakers of every quality would have us believe their wine is perfectly balanced, has a great finish, and so on. The truth is, only a miniscule fraction of the world's wine has 'great balance', and unfortunately Sula's Cabernet/Shiraz is very clearly not among them. At Rs. 395, it is not good value. AVERAGE.

✣ CABERNET/SHIRAZ (13.5%) 2005

EYE: Limpid purple of deep intensity.
NOSE: Jammy, with forest fruit. A distinct possibility of oaking.
TASTE: Dark red fruit, inky and cola-like. Too thin to be so tannic. Acid is decent and nice clove on the finish.

EVALUATION

The 2005 is much better than the 2004; however, the bottle I procured was a whopping Rs. 470. Thus, I think it is only just slipping into GOOD.

✣ MADERA RED WINE (12.5%) 2004

EYE: Very light, cherry red.
NOSE: Highly aromatic—some red liquorice, strawberries, and mandarin orange. Lovely.
TASTE: Watery, acidic, flabby, sulphuric and unpleasant.

EVALUATION

The Madera Red is, like the White, the lower end of Sula's red wine range (Rs. 205). Like the White, the Red is also a blend of classic and local Indian varieties. Sula describes it in exactly the same terms as the White: 'The wine is young, fruity and light-bodied....The bottle is beautifully packaged with the label inspired by Warli, a local tribal art form depicting rural life.' Although the label is nice, the wine is not. AVERAGE.

✣ BLUSH ZINFANDEL (12%) 2003

EYE: Salmon pink, nice looking.

NOSE: Full of sulphur, smells off, and of garbage.

TASTE: Cannot get past the sulphur. Some mandarin orange might perhaps show some nice fruit were it not for the sulphur.

EVALUATION

Rosés are hardly ever great wines, no matter where they are grown. One of the world's best is southern France's Tavel, which I wish were easily available in India. Rosés are usually always fun and refreshing wines, and are especially enjoyable in the Indian climate. Sula's wine is made from 100 per cent Zinfandel. The grape skins are left in contact with the pressed juice overnight to extract the pink colour. This is the best way to make blush wines, though most of the wines in India are simply blends of red and white wine. Sula's Blush could be something to look forward to in the future, if they take care of the sulphur problem. AVERAGE.

❖❖❖ BLUSH ZINFANDEL (12%) 2005

EYE: Slightly sparkling onion skin, watery.

NOSE: Oranges and candied strawberries with sweet ruby grapefruit.

TASTE: Get some of that candied fruit. Acid is low and thus tastes a touch too sweet.

EVALUATION

The wine is far superior to previous years. Importantly a tastes much cleaner. It is costly at Rs. 440, but it is good.

❖❖❖ MADERA ROSÉ (11.5%) 2004

EYE: Strangely far more purple than salmon, ever-so-slightly sparkling.

NOSE: Full of sulphur, thus closed—most unusually non-aromatic for local grapes.

TASTE: No complexity, no flavour, just plain straightforward fruit, with good acidity.

EVALUATION

The only remarkable thing about this wine is that

it does not repulse one in the least. That is a great achievement in comparison to Sula's other rosé. And for a mere Rs. 205, I will even go so far as to rate this one as GOOD.

CONCLUSION

Sula had been a paradox, or perhaps a classical example of how to sell widgets, that is, how to sell any product well, no matter how good. It had not been selling very good wine, but still it had been selling well. Now, thankfully, the 2005s are much superior to their earlier years—seems they bought up the right small timers. I hope they keep up this trend of improving their line. Now out of 9 wines, only one is VERY GOOD and 4 are GOOD. That is a happy improvement over previous years, when only the Sula Brut was interesting for us. Let's keep our fingers crossed for 2006.

VINBROS & CO., PONDICHERRY

23, Romain Rolland Street,
Pondicherry

This Pondicherry company dates back to 1942, primarily dealing in the liquor trade consisting of goods imported from France, Scotland, Jamaica, and Great Britain, as well as in domestic production. The company is tied up with Shaw Wallace, and makes a couple of 'wines' that are just as bad as those produced by the giant.

Like Shaw Wallace, Vinbros claims that their 'company's business concept is to satisfy customer demands in relation to the price and quality of the products offered.'

They have two wines of their own:

1. Globus Port Wine
2. Vinbros Red Magic Ruby Red Wine

GLOBUS PORT WINE

As a fortified wine, this falls outside the scope of the Wine Guide.

÷ VINBROS RED MAGIC RUBY RED WINE (NV)

EYE: A dull, well, ruby red.

NOSE: Harsh smell: earth, grime and alcohol.

TASTE: Thin and acrid, simply horrible.

EVALUATION

The wine is as astonishing as its name. It falls in the Bosca range, but for some reason costs almost twice as much (Rs. 230). POOR.

VINICOLA

....

(Costa & Co.)
248 Borda, Margao, 403602, Goa

Vinicola private limited is Goa's largest producer of wine. They have a wide range of wines that challenges even Indage in variety. However, their wines are generally of poor quality, and I think their primary aim is to produce wine of the most basic type in order to supply Asia's Catholic community, who require wine for the Sacrament. Vinicola supplies Sacramental wine to the Archdiocese in India, as well as to the dioceses of Malaysia, Papua, and Singapore. Nevertheless, they do have a wide range of wine types which is listed below.

I have not done careful tasting of Vinicola's wines, firstly, because they are not readily available outside of Goa, and secondly, because from what I have tasted, I do think these wines merit attention. I have included the list only for reference.

1. Casal Red (Slightly sparkling red wine)
2. Casal White (Slightly sparkling white wine)
3. 28 Carats Red
4. 28 Carats White (Sparkling white wine)
5. Apple Champagne (Sparkling wine made with apple extracts)
6. Sangria (Slightly sparkling sweet wine)
7. Conde de Monte Cristo (Dry white wine)
8. Adega de Velha
9. Vino Branco Doce (Sweet white wine)
10. Vinicola Riesling (Dry white wine, probably not really made with Riesling)
11. Vinicola Cabernet (Dry red wine, perhaps made from Cabernet)
12. Vinicola Muscatel (Sweet white, perhaps made from Muscat)
13. Vinicola Medallion (Dry white wine)
14. Vinicola Rosé Wine (Sweet, light pink wine)
15. Vinicola Ruby Wine

16. Granjo
17. Colva Brut

VINSURA WINES

(Sankalp Winery)
A/p Vinchur, Tal. Niphad,
Dist. Nashik, M.S.

Vinsura is probably the most exciting new domestic producer of wine. Like Sula, California winemaker Kerry Damskey is the technical consultant of Vinsura. The production equipment is all modern. M.P. Sharma is the chief winemaker, and he is pumping out large volumes of wine annually. Vinsura has the (impossibly) ambitious goal of producing as many as 110,000 cases annually by the end of 2005. If they are in earnest about this, it is saddening news: increase in quantity will certainly decrease quality. And it is quality that we all pray for with Indian wines.

But in truth, I doubt if Vinsura will be going in that direction. The big problem that any new quality winery faces in India is breaking into the market, which is entirely controlled by Indage, followed by Sula and Grover. These big companies can be ruthless, forcing the smaller wineries to sell their product to them and to agree not to market their own winery as long as the big brother is buying their wines. This is a severe blow to the small wineries, because without marketing they will get nowhere.

Vinsura wines are the product of Sankalp Winery Private Ltd., which is run by Khadangle (a chemist), K. Holkar (a horticulturist), and Nathe (a management expert). Sankalp management claim to have a clear vision, direction, and purpose for their enterprise, and I wish them all the very best in their endeavour to produce high quality Indian wines. Right now they are making one or two of India's best. If they get lucky, and escape from the pressure that Indage might be exerting upon them, and find a market of their own, they will surely be India's premier wine brand.

Vinsura has a range of classical wines, with the Cabernet Sauvignon, Zinfandel and Syrah varieties grown for the red wines, and Sauvignon Blanc, Chenin Blanc and (little known, not noble) Symphony grown for the whites.

++++ CHENIN BLANC (12%) 2003

EYE: Light bronze with yellow-green streaks.
NOSE: Lifted papaya and melon.
TASTE: Hit first by sweetness, followed by a clean

mineral touch, some disturbing ethyl alcohol, but then some lovely crisp acid at the finish.

EVALUATION

The perfect acidity more than compensates for the mild over-sweetness. Although the alcohol is unpleasant in the back of the mouth, the wine as a whole is, at Rs. 350, VERY GOOD.

❖❖❖ ZINFANDEL (14%) 2004

EYE: Purplish red of medium intensity with orange streaks.

NOSE: Lovely nose, perfume, rose, raspberry, blueberry, and Zinfandel character (plum, clove), though one does get hit a bit by the alcohol.

TASTE: Balance leans toward acid and alcohol, insufficiently tannic, but pleasant and very fruity.

EVALUATION

I wish it were richer and more intense (I think they did not want to risk offending the Indian palate with too much tannin), but at least it is very clean. This is a wine to watch. If Vinsura decides to leave the juice in contact with the skins somewhat longer, this could be one of India's top wines. Even now, for Rs. 400, it is GOOD.

❖❖❖ ROSÉ (12%) 2004

EYE: Salmon pink, some sediment and some froth.

NOSE: Highly perfumed with some candied fruit, no sulphur dioxide for a change.

TASTE: Very rich, slightly sweet with almost enough acid.

EVALUATION

This coral-pink wine is a blend of an undisclosed white varietal with Cabernet Sauvignon. According to the resident poet of Vinsura, 'It is smooth, straight forward, pleasant and easy to drink. It has noticeable residual sugar and hence, a good choice to be enjoyed with spicy Indian cuisine. It is ideal with fast food and snacks. It could also be the choice of people who would like to be introduced to wine appreciation.' I think this time I would more or less agree, especially for Rs. 360. GOOD.

+/++ FLORA (12.5%) 2003

EYE: Surprisingly pale and clear.
NOSE: Hint of lychee and jasmine.
TASTE: Flabby, completely without structure, and too sweet.

EVALUATION

This is made from the so-called Symphony grape, which is either an indigenous grape, a table grape, or some newly created hybrid. The description is that it is 'a Symphony-blend, retaining freshness and flavours of its constituents.' That suggests that 'Symphony' refers to blending and not to a grape variety, but this is some kind of mix-up. What has been blended? They continue: 'Flora is a full-bodied wine with a clean structure, spicy flavours, notes of raspberries, fresh tropical fruits and excellent notes of spring flowers, rounding off to a memorable finish. It is enjoyable with a wide variety of dishes and does not particularly require careful matching'. Unfortunately, these are empty words. Flora is somewhere between POOR and AVERAGE, and since it is the company's most expensive wine (Rs. 400), for some inexplicable reason, I am inclined to rate it lower.

++ SAUVIGNON BLANC (13%) 2003

EYE: Slightly cloudy, tinged with lemon-gold.
NOSE: Very green, an overload of spicy paprika, with a touch of plum.
TASTE: Full and acidic with a dry finish.

EVALUATION

The resident poet who has created the labels has become more technically descriptive with the Sauvignon Blanc: 'This is a unique winemaking concept. The clusters are harvested by hand at the right stage of ripeness and then fermented in stainless still vessels at 15°. The wine thus created is light, dry, and has herbaceous grassy characteristic. It performs its role as light refreshment too well. It compliments with seafood and a wide variety of gently spicy Indian dishes including chicken, pasta, and continental dishes.' I especially like the part about it performing its role as a refreshment too well! Anyway, this is not one of Vinsura's finer achievements, but it is not bad either. It is costly, though, at Rs. 395, and thus one cannot justify giving it more than AVERAGE.

CONCLUSION

Last but far from least, as mentioned, Vinsura is a brand to watch. Soon they will release a Shiraz, and I eagerly wait for it to hit the market so I can try it. In terms of inherent quality, Vinsura is outperforming all the biggies, and to match that, they even have nice front labels – they haven't, therefore, made N.D.'s mistake. However, the back labels could do with a reworking. All in all, Vinsura is a good new winery poised for take off.

Other Wineries
(CURRENTLY BEING DEVELOPED)

I mentioned at the beginning of Part Two that not all Indian wineries have been included, as some of them produce such abhorrent plonk that their product can scarcely be called "wine." In addition to these, there is yet another class of winery that has not made it into the book: those which are just starting, which have not yet got wines on the market. And finally, there is yet another brand that did not make it into Part Two, this time because it is actually marketed by a distributor and not by the producer of the wine. In this final section of Part Two, first we will quickly deal with this last-mentioned anomaly, and then list the new wineries that are only now coming into operation.

J & P WINE CONNOISSEUR

J & P is a distributor, and they have bought Cabernet Sauvignon from N.D. Wines and bottled it as a sort of health product—Heart Care. It is an interesting idea, since part of the current Indian wine boom is a result of health consciousness of the Indian middle class, who are learning that red wine can be good for your health.

EYE: Intense red, but nevertheless rather watery edges.

NOSE: Pronounced cheddar cheese, burnt rubber, yeast and capsicum.

TASTE: Thin, a decent tannin coating, some berry character, but very chemical, sulphur dioxide. Also somewhat green.

EVALUATION

The wine gets much, much better after a good 20 minutes of breathing. The main problem with the wine is that there must have been some trouble with mercaptans during fermentation, and the brew was treated with too much sulphur. It is just too chemical, but again, with breathing this tones down. I would suggest buying from N.D. Wines instead, since it is more likely that the bottle was properly handled. At Rs. 360, the wine is GOOD.

KIARA WINES

Kiara Wines is a nicely labelled bottling of Blue Star Agro's products. I believe they have only around 30,000 bottles to move, but in case you see Kiara on the shelves, let me give some details. First, Kiara has one red wine (Shiraz) and two whites (Chenin Blanc and Sauvignon Blanc). The wines are above average, for sure, and you can check the tasting notes for them above in the section on Bluefolds (Blue Star Agro). One problem is that Kiara prices its wines higher than Bluefolds does for the same product.

NEW WINERIES

Now, the following wineries have either not yet produced any wine, or they have produced some, which are not yet bottled. I have listed them here because there is every likelihood that one or two of them will produce good-quality wines. So, whenever you are shopping for new wines to try, look out for any of these:

GIRANA VALLEY WINE YARD
A/p. Bhaoor, Tal. Deola, Dist. Nashik, MS

INDOGRAPE WINERY
A/p. Gopalpur, Tal. Pandharpur, Dist. Solapur, MS

KALYANI WINES AND BEVERAGES
Maya Hospital, Mayni Road, A/p. Vita, Tal. Khanapur, Dist. Sangli, MS

MAHARAJA WINERY (SAKI)
Arogya Vignon Vidyapeeth, A/p. Dhakambe Shivar, Tal. Dindori, Dist. Nashik, MS

MOHINI WINERIES
Gat No. 321, A/p. Akolekati, Tal. North Solapur, Dist. Solapur, MS

SAHAYADRI HILLS VINEYARDS
271 Samrajya, Sangliwadi, Dist. Sangli, MS

SHIVPRASAD WINES
Kakasaheb Wagnagar, A/p. Ranwad, Tal. Niphad, Dist. Nashik, MS

Part III

INTERNATIONAL WINES

A COMPLETE GUIDE FOR INDIA

WINES OF THE WORLD

An Overview

This part of the wine guide concentrates on the wines of those regions that often show up on the Indian market, either for sale in shops or widely available at restaurants and hotels in India.

Part Three is divided into two main sections: (i) international wines in overview; and (ii) an evaluation of each imported wine widely available on the Indian market. Section (i) will itself have several sub-sections, that is, each of the important wine-growing nations, and the main specific regions within them. Section (ii) will also have two main sub-sections: (a) wines imported and bottled, distributed or sold by India's domestic producers; and, (b) wine imported and distributed by the international producer itself.

EUROPEAN WINES

Wine is often classified as being new world or old world. These terms are pretty skewed, since for example this formula requires that Indian wine be placed in the new world while German wine be placed in the old world. There are other even more important reasons why this classification is not useful, but I have mentioned it because you will hear it often. The countries falling under the new world heading include the USA, Chile, Australia, and South Africa. Countries falling under the old world heading include France, Germany, Italy, and Spain. We will usually call the old-world wines European wine, and within European wines, the best place to begin is France.

The Wines of
FRANCE

Many people regard French wines as the best in the world and this belief is even shared by countries that compete with France. The general statement 'French wines are the best' makes little sense now as wines as good as French wines are produced all around the world. However, it is true that the country does produce many of the finest world wines, and with so many different growing regions within the country, there seems to be a wine to suit anyone.

French wine is already available on the Indian market. Georges Duboeuf's wines (including Beaujolais) are plentiful, and Albert Bichot's range of wines are also available. As mentioned in Part Two, Indage buys bulk wine from Bordeaux and bottles and sells it in India.

The main areas of wine production in France that you should be familiar with are Bordeaux, Burgundy, Beaujolais, Champagne, Loire, and the Rhône. Actually, it is enough to know Bordeaux, Burgundy (which includes Beaujolais) and Champagne, which everyone is familiar with. I have mentioned Loire and the Rhône because the Loire region, with its castles and rolling hills, is very typical French wine-country, and it also happens to make wines that go best with Indian food. Rhône is mentioned because of its very famous wine, Chateauneuf-du-Pape, which everyone should know about, as it is, indeed, one of the greatest affordable wines in the world.

BORDEAUX

Bordeaux, near the Atlantic coast, is in the south-west of France. This is the most famous quality wine producing region of France. It runs along the Dordogne and Garonne Rivers from the city of Bordeaux downstream to the Atlantic coast. It is the home of some of the world's greatest wines, generally made from Cabernet Sauvignon blended with Merlot, and sometimes with other minor grapes, especially one called Cabernet Franc.

Bordeaux wines from the delimited (i.e., legally specified) sub-regions, such as from the Medoc and Haut-Medoc, down to such specific villages as Pauillac and Margaux, are considered the most desirable. Wines from the right bank of the river, such as St. Emilion and Pomerol, often contain higher proportions of Merlot (you will learn about these sub-regions below). So, basically, if someone gifts you a bottle of red wine from Bordeaux, you can bet it will contain Cabernet Sauvignon and/or Merlot, even though it is surely not going to tell you this on the label as it is illegal!

The French have a highly regulated wine industry that covers everything right down to what you can write on your wine labels, and the name of the grape is not usually permitted on what are called AOC wines. AOC stands for *appellation d'origine contrôllée*, or controlled name of origin: both the name and the origin are controlled. All French wines go under testing to determine if they live up to certain standards, and those that do, which have properties that can be identified as being wine from a certain origin, are granted AOC status.

All AOC wines will have *appellation contrôllée* marked clearly on the label.

There are other rankings below that of AOC, like VDQS (in English, wines of superior quality) and *vin de pays* (VDP, or country wine). If you are handed a bottle of French wine that does not state AOC, VDQS or VDP on the label, hand it back.

Bordeaux has 57 appellations, that is, specific names of AOC status. It has more than 9,000 wine-producing chateaux, and 13,000 wine growers. This is why the Bordeaux region is one of the most important wine producing regions in the world, and it produces a third of the good quality French production.

Wine has been grown in Bordeaux for 2,000 years. Most probably vines grew there before the arrival of the Romans in 56 BC. During British occupation of the Bordeaux region, from 1154-1453, numerous ships stocked with Bordeaux wine regularly embarked for England. The wine was far lighter then than the typical red velvety colour we expect today, and it was called 'claret'. Even today, the British refer to red Bordeaux wine as claret.

I have mentioned the red wine grapes of this region already. To repeat, most of the grapes grown in the Bordeaux for red wine are Cabernet Sauvignon, which gives vigour, tannin, and good ageing qualities, and Merlot, which brings softness and suppleness. In the Bordeaux white wines you will find primarily Sauvignon Blanc and Semillon.

The best known appellations in Bordeaux are as follows:

Medoc: Appellation Medoc wines are red. They are delicate, medium coloured, fine and elegant; often tannic when young, harmonious and splendid when matured. The Medoc is situated north of the town of Bordeaux. It is divided into the Haut-Medoc in the south, near the town, and the northern part, which is traditionally simply called Medoc. Haut-Medoc is the homeland of the most famous vineyards in the world; it is divided into smaller areas called 'communes'.

Going from north to south, the first one is Saint-Estèphe. Its wines are very coloured, earthy, firm, robust, and tannic. They reach their maturity slower than other Medoc wines. In Pauillac you will find Chateau Lafite, Chateau Latour, and Chateau Mouton-Rothschild. The wines generally have a lot of body; tannic and acid when young, these wines have an opulent bouquet with aromas of blackcurrant and cedar when aged.

Saint-Julien wines are much lighter and very aromatic. They are harmonious and well balanced. Moulis and Listrac generally produce dry and fruity wines, ready to drink sooner than other Medoc wines. In Margaux, the famous Chateau Margaux produces the most delicate wines of the Medoc. They have a perfumed bouquet and a magnificent elegance.

The other well-known Bordeaux wines are from Graves. This area gets its name from its gravelly soil. It is located just outside the town of Bordeaux. The red wines of Graves are recognizable by their garnet-red colour, rich, attractive, and more robust than the other Medoc wines. You will find Chateau Haut-Brion in Graves. Two thirds of Graves wines are white. They are generally fresh, fruity, and dry.

Saint-Emilion is another famous Bordeaux name. Located 30 kilometres north of Bordeaux, Saint-Emilion is the oldest viticultural area of the region. Its wines are intensely coloured, and generally reach their maturity quicker than the other red Bordeaux.

Pomerol is a relatively new but very sought-after wine. Pomerol is the smallest wine-producing area in the Bordeaux region. Its wines can be more robust and hardy than others from the area. They have an exquisite velvety quality. The most famous vineyard is Pétrus.

In the southern Bordeaux region, Sauternes and Barsac are famous for their exceptional sweet, golden wines. They are among the best dessert wines in the world. The world-famous names include Yquem, Raymond-Lafon and Rieussec in Sauternes, and Climens and Coutet in Barsac. These sweet wines are made from the Semillon grapes that have undergone noble-rot.

Noble-rot is quite a funny term, but it is an important phenomenon. More technically, it is called *botrytis cinerea*. It is a mould that grows on the grapes that sucks out all the water leaving them dry and shrivelled up. What is left in the grape is the most concentrated, sweet nectar, and when grapes affected by noble-rot are pressed, the wine produced out of this rich must is deliciously sweet and complex. Noble-rotted grapes are necessary to make the rich, sweet wines of Sauternes in France as well as the German Beerenauslese and Trockenbeerenauslese wines, which are discussed later.

Earlier I had stated that you really only need to know about Bordeaux, Burgundy, and Champagne, but I did also mention the Loire and Rhône regions. I am going to introduce you to the Loire now, after Bordeaux, because they share a certain resemblance. That is, if you pick up a French wine and the label has the word Chateau (castle) on it, then it is most likely going to be from Bordeaux or the Loire. You can also bet that it will not be from Burgundy, but we will get to that area a bit later.

LOIRE

The valley of the Loire, in central-west France, is sometimes regarded as the most beautiful French wine region. The Loire River is wide and deep, and the landscape quiet and undulating. It is said that the wines reflect the mood of the landscape. They are soft, pleasant, charming, and light. About three-quarters of the wine production in the Loire is white wine. Loire wines go very well with Indian food as the crisp acidity of the wines balance out the sting of strong spices.

The greatest share of high-quality Loire whites are made from the Sauvignon Blanc grape. But the Chenin Blanc is the main variety of white grape which is grown. As for the famous names from here, let me mention just a few. First the Pouilly and Sancerre. The delicious, dry white Pouilly-Fumé has a bewitching perfume—asparagus and flint—and a distinctive smokey flavour (*fumé* actually means smoked). It is a highly regulated production: it must only be made from the Sauvignon grape; must have a minimum natural alcohol content of 11 per cent; and production is limited to 990 gallons per acre. The Sancerre is produced on the opposite bank of the river from Pouilly. The white wine is very dry, and also quite fruity—most importantly, it should be drunk young. Sancerres are made with Sauvignon Blanc.

Touraine is also the homeland of the best red Loire wines, Bourgueil and Chinon, made mainly from the grape Cabernet Franc. This grape is also largely used with Cabernet Sauvignon and Merlot in the Bordeaux region. The whites from Touraine use Chenin Blanc.

BURGUNDY

Everyone has heard of the wines of Burgundy, they have always been among the world's best, and for the last couple of decades, they have commanded the world's highest prices. Clearly some of the most exciting wines in the world come from this region. Generally, Burgundy reds are velvety and subtle, while the whites are sensual and characteristically full bodied. Burgundy produces two of the most popular wines of France: Beaujolais and Chablis. We will treat Beaujolais at the end of this section.

Burgundy (Bourgogne, in French, which is the word you are more likely to see on the label) begins 100 kilometres south from Paris and spreads down to the city of Lyon. Thus, the wine-region stretches on for 360 kilometres. It is a region with various soils, and divided into numerous districts: Chablis, Côte d'Or (itself divided into Côte de Nuits and Côte de Beaune), Côte Chalonnaise, Mâconnais and Beaujolais. Again, the regions of Chablis and Beaujolais are the ones to remember.

The production of wine began here with the invasion of the Romans. Later, during the sixth century, one of the nearby kings gave his vineyards to the church. At the time of the French Revolution, most of the best Burgundy wines were produced by monasteries.

One of the consequences of the French Revolution was the confiscation of the vineyards from the church and their fragmentation into innumerable small plots. Nowadays, the system of small vineyards still prevails in Burgundy. This is why I said that you will probably never find a Burgundy labelled Chateau, like Bordeaux and Loire often are.

Burgundy red wines are made from the Pinot Noir grape variety, while Beaujolais wines are made from the Gamay. The Burgundy white wines are made from Chardonnay, and people like me love to drink this wine while eating snails.

Moving on to the specific territories, we start with the northern-most, Chablis. The village of Chablis produces the white wine of the same name, one of the most famous in France. It is light-coloured, pale and dry, and the perfect balance masks the high acidity. Chablis is grown on chalky clay over limestone soil, which is supposed to be the best soil for the Chardonnay grape.

Then comes the Côte de Nuits which is situated just south of Dijon. Red Côte de Nuits are soft, smooth and velvety, with acidity for backbone and longevity. Their bouquet is intense with truffles, violets, and raspberries. The most famous villages producing Côte de Nuits are Chambertin and Vosne-Romanée (where you find Romanée-Conti, the most expensive wine in the world).

The Côte de Beaune begins just a few kilometres south from Nuits Saint-Georges. Red Côte de Beaune are noticeable for their warm bouquet (another word for *nose* or the smell of the wine). They have a tendency toward a slightly lighter body and a quicker maturation than the Côtes de Nuits. The white wines are straw-yellow, robust, smooth, and very dry.

The viticultural centre of this area is the famous village of Beaune. The Hospices de Beaune, a charity hospital founded in 1443, is located here. The Hospices wines are auctioned every year just after the harvest. It is one of the major events of the French wine calendar.

Then come Côte Châlonnaise and Mâcon, but I will only mention the most famous wine from these, which is Pouilly-Fuissé, from Mâcon (this should not be confused with Pouilly-Fumé from the Loire).

Now down to Beaujolais, the last district of Burgundy. Although Beaujolais does fall within the Burgundy region, since its wine (and grape variety) differs so radically from Burgundy wines, most books treat Beaujolais as a region in itself. It produces one of the most famous red wines in the world. Beaujolais takes its light and fruity flavour from the Gamay grape variety. This is one of the few red wines that is generally served chilled (the Bourgueil and Chinon from the Loire are the other two), like white wines.

There are four categories of wines in Beaujolais, but knowing this is strictly for the experts, so you can refer to it later:

(1) Cru Beaujolais. These cru, or growths, are special villages that produce top quality wines. Their names are, Brouilly, Côte de Brouilly, Morgon, Chénas, Chiroubles, Fleurie, Juliénas, Moulin à Vent, Régnié, and Saint Amour, where the granite provides a great soil for the Gamay grape.

(2) Beaujolais in the northern part of the district, where the soil is limestone. This is the simplest, and will be sold as Beaujolais AOC, without any other specific name on the label.

(3) Beaujolais Supérieur is in the same part of the district, but it differs from the regular Beaujolais because it has one degree more of alcohol. Generally, when a wine label has the word Supérieur on it, for example, Bordeaux Supérieur, it means that

the wine has one more degree of alcohol than the typical AOC, or in our example, than Bordeaux AOC.

(4) Beaujolais-Village. This is a Beaujolais coming from one of the 39 listed villages. On the label will be Beaujolais-Village AOC, instead of just Beaujolais AOC.

This is very advanced information, and is here for those of you who wish to go deeper into the issue.

To summarize, Burgundy is Bourgogne in French. The red wines from Burgundy are made with the Pinot Noir grape, while the whites with the Chardonnay grape. This does not include Beaujolais, which is made from Gamay.

CHAMPAGNE

The last region in France that you must know about is one that you would have already heard of, Champagne. The wine from this region was so popular that basically all wine that looks like it, that is, that bubbles, is called by its name. In France itself, it is illegal to call a sparkling wine Champagne unless it is actually from the region (remember the AOC regulations, where the name of origin is controlled?). However, in the rest of the world, at least until the 1990s, sparkling wine was called Champagne, although now the French have successfully lobbied most countries to prevent this hijacking of their prized name.

Sparkling wine that is made outside of Champagne and outside of France, if made in the same way as the French Champagne, that is, using a traditional process in which the wine gains its sparkle by a secondary fermentation in the bottle, is labelled as 'Sparkling wine made by the traditional method', that is, *methode traditionelle*, or *methode champenoise*. India's once-famous Omar Khayyam is made through the highly demanding and expensive Champagne method.

Champagne is expensive by any standards. This is largely because of the production cost involved, and the huge demand for it. It is a wonderful style of wine, and it is a joy to drink. No celebration in the West is complete without Champagne, or at least, without sparkling wine. But remember, the less expensive sparkling wine is, the less likely it is to have been made through the traditional method, and thus, the lower the quality is likely to be. In Champagne and sparkling wine, quality generally quite accurately translates into cost.

Champagnes come in several styles, the most basic distinctions of which include white or rosé, vintage or non-vintage, or dry or sweet. Let me deal with these distinctions first.

A Champagne's colour can vary from pale gold to green gold, from amber to yellow gold, from old gold to grey gold. All these differences reveal a lot about the wine's character, the length of time it has been aged, and the grapes that have been used. A light wine will be a clear colour, whereas a powerful wine will be darker. White wines (including Champagnes) darken with age.

Rosé Champagnes are alluring, and are usually obtained by adding red wine to white wine. The pleasure we derive from them is aesthetic and psychological, since their tint evokes tender feelings, and this is why they are often the chosen wine for romantic moments. Just like the whites, their colour may range from light to dark, and their flavours from the lightest and most elegant through to the most full-bodied.

Most Champagne is non-vintage, which means that they result from a blend of various harvest years. Every year a proportion of the harvest is reserved for future blends. It is with this reserve that the winemaker is able to create the same style every year. Thus, a non-vintage wine is said to show the house (Champagne-maker's) style.

On the other hand, vintage Champagne is created when a harvest has exceptional character and deserves to be appreciated to the full. Thus, it is not every year when the winemaker produces a vintage wine. These tend to be costlier than the non-vintage house-brand.

Dry Champagnes are called brut while sweeter ones are called demi-sec, which literally means half-dry. More sugar is added to demi-sec Champagnes than to brut Champagnes during production. This is what gives them their sweet taste. One should only serve a sweet champagne (that is, demi-sec) during dessert, otherwise, brut is the typical champagne served.

Despite these distinctions, Champagne is made according to a specific tradition that characterizes all the wines from the region. Traditionally, the wines are blends from different growing areas. Again, there are only three permitted grape varieties—Pinot Noir, Pinot Meunier, and Chardonnay—each of which imparts its own character: power for Pinot Noir, fruitiness for Pinot Meunier, and finesse for Chardonnay.

Traditional brut or demi-sec Champagnes are made using the three varieties and they strive for a balance of power, fruit, and finesse. Equally, they can be dominated by one of the three varieties. This type of information is usually not visible on the label.

There are some other fine distinctions, which you will see on the label. You might read there, 'Blanc de Blancs' or 'Blanc de Noir'.

A Blanc de Blancs Champagne is made by using only the Chardonnay grape and is characterized by its finesse. A Blanc de Noir Champagne uses Pinot Noir and/or Pinot Meunier grapes, and is characterized by either power or fruitiness, sometimes both together. This means that when white Champagne is made from only black grapes, it is called Blanc de Noir, and when it is made only from white grapes, it is called Blanc de Blancs. Most often Champagne is made from a blend, and rosé Champagne must, of course, come from at least some black grapes in order to get its colour.

What else might you find on the typical Champagne label?

You will, of course, find the alcohol content, the region (Champagne), and the bottle volume, and more importantly, you will see the producer's name. Now, all of this information will be on any and every bottle of wine, whether from Champagne or Tasmania. On a Champagne bottle, then, you will also find whether the wine is dry (brut), very dry (extra brut), or sweet (demi-sec), and perhaps the special name for that particular Champagne, such as Prestige, or some other fancy title. This is the name that the producer has given to that particular blend of grapes and length of ageing and so on.

Some of the best-known producer names in Champagne include Veuve Clicquot, Krug, Bollinger, Taittinger, Piper-Heidsieck, and of course, Moet & Chandon, who make one of the most famous Champagnes called Dom Perignon, named after the monk (Dom Perignon) who is said to have discovered Champagne. There are numerous myths surrounding Perignon, and his alleged discovery of Champagne is among the most persistent.

RHÔNE

Champagne is one of the most wonderful drinks on the planet. Unfortunately, only the rich get to enjoy it. But the wines of the Rhône valley are another story—everyone can have a chance at these wines, since it is produced in large quantities, some of it not too great, while some is truly wonderful.

The Rhône is a southern French wine region running along the river of the same name. It is best known for its hearty reds based on Syrah, but also mixed with other lesser varieties. It has a winemaking history certainly going back to the fourteenth century, and more likely all the way back to the Romans. The Rhône is divided into the southern Rhône and the northern Rhône.

My personal favourite wine from the southern Rhône is called Chateauneuf-du-Pape. This is an excellent, complex dry red wine made from a blend of up to 13 specified grapes and boasting a heritage that reaches back to the fourteenth century sojourn of the Catholic Popes in nearby Avignon, when they split with Rome. The name of this wine means 'new castle of the Pope'.

Other great wines from the southern Rhône include Gigondas. These are very similar in style to Chateauneuf-du-Pape but cost less. Tavel has the reputation of being the best rosé wine in France, and in my opinion, in the world. It is made from a blend of up to ten varieties, but Grenache predominates. The wine is strong, often above 12 per cent, and can be drunk with a very wide range of foods, including meats. It is a full, fruity wine best drunk between three to five years old.

Finally, the southern vineyards produce 80 per cent of Côtes du Rhône wines. These wines are produced in large quantity and are considered good value for everyday consumption.

Things start getting more expensive in the northern vineyards. Here you find the Côte Rôtie, with its hills bathed (or rather *roasted*, which is where the name comes from) in the sun, which produces a warm, robust, full-bodied, richly-coloured red wine. Harsh and dark when they are young, these wines become softer and develop an excellent bouquet with age. The Syrah grape dominates the production.

Another famous wine, also expensive, is Hermitage. The Hermitage reds are generous, well balanced, and strongly aromatic. They age remarkably well, for 50 years and more, and become smooth and mellow when they mature. Here, too, Syrah is the main variety used, often softened by up to 15 per cent with two lesser-known white varieties (Marsanne and Roussanne).

Thus ends the introduction to the French wines. We treated the famous wine-growing regions of Bordeaux, Loire, Champagne, Burgundy (including Beaujolais), and the Rhône. Before moving on to other European countries, at least a mention should be made of the other wine-producing areas of France, because there is wine now available on the Indian market from French regions not discussed above.

First, there is Alsace. Wines produced in Alsace are in some respects more similar to German wines than to their French counterparts, with the exception that most wines produced in

Alsace are dry, whereas most of those produced in Germany—as you are about to learn—are sweet. Riesling is the primary grape used for quality wines in Alsace.

Next, the wines of the Midi can be great value. If you can get your hands on a red Corbieres or Minervois, then be sure to try it. They are ordinary drinking wines, but generally good quality and less expensive.

Finally, I want to draw your attention once again to the system of classifying French wines, in order to mention the vin de pays rung. Within the VDP, there is now a very popular everyday sort of drinking wine coming out of d'Oc—Vin de pays d'Oc. Since these come for as little as $2 (Rs. 100) a bottle in Europe, they are very popular for daily consumption. The quality of some of them is exceptional, especially considering the price. Some VDP d'Oc wines are already on the Indian market, although, of course, they do not cost Rs. 100 but rather something like Rs. 1000. Nevertheless, find the cheapest ones and taste it.

The Wines of
GERMANY

German wines are rising in popularity, both within Europe and internationally. I also believe that these wines will invade the Indian market in the coming years, since they are thirst-quenching, light but delicious, and white wines go well with Indian foods. Already available are some Rieslings from the German firm Henkell (who also sell a pretty decent sparkling wine, called *Sekt*, explained later), and as already discussed, Indage also buys Riesling wines in bulk from Germany and bottles and distributes them in India.

While we dealt extensively with only three or four main wine regions in France, there are 13 such major regions in Germany. However, not all of them are important, and I will concentrate only on three or four of the best. But before going on to the wine regions, I should mention something about the wine classification system of Germany.

People say you need a degree in enology (the academic study of wine) in order to decipher a German wine label. Personally I do not find them terribly challenging, but I will discuss how they should be read, for those who might encounter one.

On every bottle you will find the Vintage. Vintages since 1988 have been very good, with 1990, 1994, and 2001 standing out as excellent. Other very good vintages included 1989, 1993, 1995, 1996, 1999, and 2002.

You will naturally also find the winery or estate name on the label. Some of the best established estates in Germany are Prüm, Fritz Haag, von Hövel, and Reinhold Haart, just to name a few. However, there are also the new stars such as the Robert Weil, Franz Künstler, and Gunderloch Estates. These three estates have been offering stiff competition for the greatest names in German winemaking for several years now.

Unlike in France, Germany permits mentioning the kind of grapes used on the label. What a relief! There are many different grape varieties grown in Germany, but the most popular are Riesling, Müller-Thurgau, and Silvaner. The best wines are made from the Riesling grape, and that is what we shall concentrate upon.

The most challenging part of the label, is the classification. This is where German wine can get confusing. But hopefully this explanation will clear things up. There are two major quality wine categories: (1) QbA (Qualitätswein bestimmter Anbaugebiete); and, (2) QmP (Qualitätswein mit Prädikat).

QbA is the lower category of German wine, but not the lowest. Below QbA comes Landwein, which is like France's VDP, although the latter is more reliable quality than the former. The lowest category is called tafelwein, which means ordinary wine not showing any special characteristics.

QmP is where the highest quality wines from Germany can be found. But not all QmP wines are high quality, just as not all AOC wines in France are of high quality. Sadly many of these highest classified wines in both France and Germany are of poor to average quality.

What is special about QmP wines is that they are completely natural and are bottled according to the level of sugar in the grape at harvest (when it was picked). The winemaker must only use what nature provides them in the grape, nothing else. What ends up in the bottle all revolves around a very tedious harvest system. The estate will go out into the vineyards approximately four to six times, over a period of about eight weeks selecting their grapes. These four to six selections result in batches of grapes all having varying levels of ripeness. It is these different ripeness levels which determine how the QmP wines will be bottled/labelled.

Ripeness, in this instance, is not a qualitative assessment. It is an assessment regarding the weight of the wine. Essentially what the QmP system is doing is dividing German wines into varying weight categories. In other words, it gives you a series of light, medium, and heavier weight/body wines to enjoy. To understand the term weight or body, you can compare wine with milk. Drink a glass each of non-fat milk, low-fat milk, and full-fat milk or cream. You will hopefully notice that there is a decidedly different level of weight in the mouth between each of them. That is what is called 'body' in wine terms.

However, body is just one of the many dimensions that defines a wine, and in addition, the degree to which a wine is light-bodied or heavy-bodied does not make the wine better or worse.

So the real question is, how do you tell the different weight/body groupings apart from one another? Believe it or not, every bottle of German QmP wine has this information on the label. In my opinion, this along with the fact that the grape is mentioned serves to make German labels quite approachable, but you just have to know how the rating scale works.

The weight/body of QmP wines is categorized each by a different name. The full English translation of QmP is quality wine with a predicate, and each of the levels listed below is called a predicate:

Kabinett. The first level of ripeness, these grapes produce the lightest of the QmP wines.

Spätlese. This means late harvest, which results in a medium level of ripeness, and makes a medium weight wine.

Auslese. This means specially selected, and is thus usually later harvest, making medium to heavy-weight wines.

Beerenauslese. This you will rarely see. Usually referred to as 'BA'. This is a wine made from individual berries carefully hand-selected, and makes a heavy-bodied wine.

Trockenbeerenauslese. This is a miracle. Usually referred to as 'TBA'. This is a wine made from individually selected dried berries, those which have undergone the noble-rotting described earlier while discussing the Sauternes wines. It makes a very heavy-bodied wine.

Eiswein. This is a special term given to wines whose bunches were harvested while they were frozen. It must by law have the body of at least a 'BA'. Eiswein can be more concentrated than a TBA, and are very expensive.

Now, if you look on any bottle of German QmP wine you will see one of these harvest levels noted. Remember that they only indicate the approximate 'body' of the wine, and not its quality.

The basic premise behind the German QbA and QmP system is to indicate that greater care went into the selecting and making of a QmP wine than into a QbA wine. In this respect, QmP in Germany is like AOC in France, and QbA is like VDQS. Then Landwein would be like the French VDP.

On any German label you will also notice the name of the vineyard where the grapes used to make the wine were grown. In addition to this, you will see, usually in bigger letters, the growing region or district. There are many growing regions; however, the most popular are probably the Mosel-Saar-Ruwer, Rheinhessen, Rheingau, and Pfalz, which are described below. It will also be necessary to discuss the wine regions that fall within the German state of Baden-Wuerttemberg, because of the organized lobby that this state has, pushing its wine through German embassies throughout the world.

Some German wines, the best ones, have what is called the V.D.P. Logo, which is an image of an eagle stamped onto the seal of the wine. When we talked about the different QmP categories, the problem was that you had no way to recognize the quality of the wine. Well, this logo on German wines is as close as you can get to a 'quality assurance' indicator. This eagle represents membership in the V.D.P., an elite group of winemaking estates in Germany. Of the more than 35,000 labels produced in Germany, only about 180 are V.D.P. members. This is an excellent way to begin your search for better German winemaking estates.

So, that covers everything you need to know about the German wine label. Let us move on to the wine regions.

As stated, Germany has 13 wine-growing regions, which are: Ahr, Baden, Franken, Hessische Bergstrasse, Mittelrhein, Mosel-Saar-Ruwer, Nahe, Pfalz, Rheingau, Rheinhessen, Wuerttemberg, Saale-Unstrut, and Sachsen (Saxony). The last two are in the former East Germany, while the rest are in south-western Germany.

As already mentioned, we will deal with the best of these: Mosel-Saar-Ruwer, Rheinhessen, Rheingau, and Pfalz as well as Baden and Wuerttemberg.

MOSEL-SAAR-RUWER
Wine has a very long history in Germany, dating back to the Roman settlements. Indeed, long before even the great wines of Bordeaux were classified, for many years some of the great vineyards (such as Bernkastel and Wehlen) within Mosel-Saar-Ruwer (MSR) produced the most expensive wine in the world. Even today, although Riesling is now planted all over the world, with exceptional results in places like

Australia, it is still not possible to find Rieslings as full-flavoured and stylish as those of the MSR.

Although MSR is arguably the most top-quality Riesling region in the world today, its reputation has suffered in recent years because of the lousy, sweet plonk made from inferior grapes and undistinguished vineyards. Lower predicates (these refer to the different levels already discussed, like Kabinett and Spätlese) produce light, yet brilliantly perfumed, aromatic, and long-lived wines, showing their best when the high acidity is balanced by a touch of sweetness. Fully dry wines from here can be stunning, but, except a few of the best producers, are too often harsh and thin tasting. The rare dessert wines can reach the sublime, ranking firmly among the greatest wines money can buy. Prices are often surprisingly fair, given the production costs here, where you find some of the steepest slopes for vine growing on earth.

The region of MSR spreads out over 12,000 hectares, and is planted with about 54 per cent Riesling, 21 per cent Muller-Thurgau, and 9 per cent Elbling. You should only go for the Riesling.

The best way to select an MSR is by the producer. If none of the following producers are available, then go for the vineyards listed below. First, here are the best producers: Fritz Haag, Dr. Loosen, Egon Müller, Joh. Jos. Prüm, and von Schubert.

The villages to look out for are: Piesport, Bernkastel, Graach, Wehlen, Ockfen, and Serrig.

RHEINHESSEN

The Rheinhessen is the largest of all the German regions, covering an area of 26,330 hectares. This means that about every fourth bottle of German wine comes from here. However, this area is largely planted with inferior grape varieties, and Riesling makes up only about 10 per cent of the total. About 25 per cent is Muller-Thurgau and 13 per cent Silvaner. This means that the very good wine coming out of Rheinhessen is only a small fraction of the mediocre and worse.

But there is good wine here, and it keeps getting better. The best is produced by Keller and Gunderloch Freiherr Heyl zu Herrnsheim, Schales, and Villa Sachsen are some other excellent producers. You can also try any QmP wine from the villages of Dalsheim, Florsheim, or Nierstein.

RHEINGAU

This great Riesling region of Germany is also one of the most beautiful places to visit in the country. With the numerous castles dotting the riverside, separated by steeply sloping vineyards, one cannot choose a better area for wine tourism. Additionally, the beautiful Cistercian monastery, Kloster Eberbach, is found here, open for tours and tastings, and is still after centuries producing delicious, good value wines. You also find one of the most famous German wines here called Schloss Johannisberg. It is, perhaps, the epitome of class to gift a bottle of Schloss Johannisberg to your host at a dinner party. But it may also lead to embarrassment, as your host will surely be serving something inferior to the guests.

Though a grand region, many critics say it is under performing and overpriced to a serious extent. In particular, this holds true for the famous noble estates, whose reputation has suffered (but not their arrogance). Still, some of the world's greatest Rieslings are made here by dedicated growers. In contrast to other regions, the Rheingau makes rather little cheap wine.

The Rheingau spreads out over a mere 3,230 hectares, and is planted with 81 per cent Riesling, 10 per cent Pinot Noir (called Spätburgunder in Germany), and 3 per cent Muller-Thurgau. Thus, it may also be worth trying the reds (Pinots) from this region, although obviously Rheingau is Riesling country.

Again, the best way to select a wine from Rheingau is to choose by producer. The best are: George Breuer, Robert Weil, Schloss Johannisberg, and Kloster Eberbach.

Vineyards to look for include: Eltville, Erbach, Rudesheim, Rauenthal, Hochheim, and Johannisberg.

PFALZ

Pfalz, also known as the Palatinate, is the second largest region in Germany, with 23,488 hectares planted. About 25 per cent is Riesling, 20 per cent Muller-Thurgau, and 11 per cent Portugieser, a lesser-known variety used in central Europe, and called Kekfrankos, for example, in Hungary. Similar to the Portugieser is Dornfelder, another red-wine grape that makes simple, everyday wines, which incidentally go very well with Indian food.

Since this region is so large, it is a source of much rubbish, yet this is also the place to look for some of the best non-Riesling wines in Germany, as well as plenty of top-class Rieslings. Dry whites can be world class, and so too can be its dessert wines. Serious red wines are being made here too, though not on the same level as the whites. They often represent better value than wines from other German regions.

The best producers are Müller-Catoir, Kurt Darting, Eugen Müller, and Weegmüller. The best villages to look out for are Forst, Deidesheim, Ruppertsberg, Wachenheim, Ungstein, and Kallstadt.

BADEN AND WUERTTEMBERG

Baden and Wuerttemberg are two separate winegrowing regions, but they both fall within the German state of Baden-Wuerttemberg, and thus I am treating them in the same sub-section. The reason I am discussing them at all is that this German state is so well organized and powerful that even though these regions do not produce wines on a par with MSR, you are more likely to try a glass of something from Baden or from Wuerttemberg long before you have tried any other quality German wine. As mentioned, Baden-Wuerttemberg pushes its wines through German embassies and consulates all around the world, and these missions often hold wine-tastings and parties sponsored by the state of Baden-Wuerttemberg.

Baden is a region of about 16,000 hectares, with 30 per cent Muller-Thurgau, 30 per cent Spätburgunder (Pinot Noir), and 10 per cent Grauburgunder (Pinot Gris/Grigio). Wuerttemberg is a region of about 11,200 hectares, planted with 25 per cent Riesling, 23 per cent Trollinger, and 16 per cent Schwarzriesling (the latter two lesser known local varieties). In addition to these two regions, other wine-producing regions also fall within the border of the state. Consequently, the state of Baden-Wuerttemberg includes many types and styles of wine, and with its efficient lobby and industrial-sized producers, you will find these wines the world over.

But what is worth drinking from here? From Baden, the most famous wines come from the Kaiserstuhl, which is the warmest growing zone within Germany. These wines have unusually great depth and warmth of fruit. The best producers are doubtlessly Dr. Heger and Seeger. The best villages include Ihringen and Bischoffingen.

As for Wuerttemberg, the region produces 40 per cent of Germany's red wines. The best of these are from Pinot Noir, called Spätburgunder here, but also worth trying are the wines made from a little-known grape called Lemberger. The best producers of the region are Graf (that means 'Count') Adelmann, Graf von Neipperg, and Fürst (meaning 'Prince') zu Hohenlohe-Oehringen. The leading villages are Kleinbottwar and Korb.

Finally, another innovation in German wine labelling that you need to be aware of is the new term 'Classic' that appear on the labels of certain wines. This trend began here in Wuerttemberg, but has spread to other regions. Bottles labelled CLASSIC indicate that only classic grape varieties have been used, planted in the best vineyard sites. Thus, along with the V.D.P. sign, a bottle labelled CLASSIC is also a good indication of quality for German wines.

REVIEW OF GERMAN WINES

It sometimes seems that learning about wines, however fun, is like learning a new language. So, to simplify things, let me review some of the basic points mentioned in this section. But before the review, let me mention another piece of information useful for decoding: when selecting a German wine, it is useful to remember that the German term for dry is 'trocken' and 'halbtrocken' means half-dry, or a bit sweet.

Germany's global recognition for production of the Riesling wine is on the increase. Although these wines have a reputation for being too sweet, Germany does make some very dry versions of Riesling for export. The German government has a regulated system for ranking their wines:

Landwein: the lowest quality level of wine (worth mentioning),

QbA: the middle level of quality, and

QmP: the highest quality level.

This information is printed on all German wine labels and makes choosing a German wine easier for international consumers. Within the QmP level there are different classes of body, which tends also to correspond with sweetness, although you can also find very dry Kabinetts, Spätleses, and even Ausleses. The levels are:

Kabinett: very ripe grapes (usually 9.5 per cent alcohol)

Spätlese: late harvested grapes

Auslese: individually picked ripe bunches of grapes usually used for dessert wines

Beerenauslese: hand-selected grapes used for sweet wines

Trockenbeerenauslese: the sweetest and most expensive German dessert wines.

There are also Eisweins, or Ice wines, which are very rich, very sweet, luscious dessert wines, and, generally, very expensive.

Finally, if you are confused about all the different rankings and ratings, and the German words and names found on bottles, the simplest way to acquire a high-quality German wine is to look for the eagle, the V.D.P. logo on the capsule, or look for the new CLASSIC labelled wines.

The Wines of
ITALY

The current international wine market contains a large amount of Italian wine. Despite being the world's biggest producer of wine, Italy only exports about a quarter of its production. Some of it, only a miniscule fraction, comes to India. The firms Castello and Zonin sell Chiantis (see below) and varietal wines like Chardonnay. In case you have forgotten, when a wine is sold on the basis of the grape rather than the place, then it is called a varietal wine.

Some Italian wine is very famous like Chianti, or what are called the Super-Tuscans. But much of Italian wine is just used to fortify the wines of other countries. Italian wines do tend to have very high quality standards, placing them among the best in the world. And, of course, they also have their own classification system. (See table on Classifications of European Wine at the end of the section.)

The classification of Italian wines is characterized by three significant factors: origin, intrinsic quality, and genuineness. The highest level is called Denominazione di Origine Controllata e Garantita or DOCG. This level is reserved for wines representing a particular geographical area, which is delimited, and there are the strictest limitations of areas and yields of wine per hectare or vineyard (as with all things, the lower quantity translates into higher quality). This level is like AOC in France and QmP in Germany.

Next comes Denominazione di Origine Controllata, DOC. This is just slightly under DOCG. The kinds of grapes used, the area of production, and so on are also fully regulated in this class. These are something like VDQS in France and QbA in Germany.

Then we have Indicazione Geografica Tipica, IGT. This is like VDP in France or Landwein in Germany. This wine will have the general characteristics of a region, but the regulations on kind of grapes used are not restrictive.

Interestingly, some of the finest wines of Italy, and certainly the most expensive, are in the IGT class, and not in DOCG. This is because the freedom to make a wine with whatever grapes one wishes permits untraditional winemakers to experiment with untraditional recipes, and many have met with great success. Most of these are known as 'Supertuscans', that is, wines from Tuscany that use grapes, generally Cabernet Sauvignon, that are not traditional in the region.

Last in the ranking is Vini da Tavola, VdT. These are simply generic wines, like Tafelwein in Germany or *vin de table* in France, not worth mentioning. Those are the rankings; now let us discuss the regions. Although there are quite a few, the most important ones are Tuscany, Piedmont, and Veneto.

TUSCANY

Five of Italy's nine DOCGs are found in Tuscany, a famously lovely landscape found on the western side of Central Italy. These are Brunello di Montalcino, Vino Nobile di Montepulciano, Chianti, Carmignano, and Vernaccia di San Gimignano. These are all, excepting Chianti, almost always delicious.

Chianti, still the domínant force in Tuscan viniculture, has ranked as the most Italian of wines for decades. This is partly because it is the most voluminous and widely sold classified wine, but also because it has a unique personality.

Since Chianti was elevated to DOCG in 1984, its production has sharply diminished and its quality has markedly improved. Chianti has several sub-districts, although only Chianti Classico, whose bottles always carry a picture of a black rooster, is widely known. Simply put, wine labelled Chianti is the lowest quality level within the DOCG rank. Then comes Chianti Classico, which are wines from the inner districts of Chianti. Highest is Chianti Classico Riserva, which is wine from a Classico area that is aged for a minimum of three years.

What Chianti has in common with all the classified red wines of Tuscany is its major grape variety: Sangiovese. In the past, varieties were often blended, but today the emphasis is strongly on Sangiovese.

From good vintages, pure Sangiovese wines are rich in body and intricate in flavour with deep ruby-garnet colours. Some are smooth and round almost from the start, but others need years to develop the nuances of bouquet and flavour unique to well-aged Tuscan reds. When conditions are not favourable, reds from Sangiovese can be lean, harsh, and bitter. That explains why some

producers have planted other varieties to complement the natives. Cabernet Sauvignon and Merlot have made progress in Tuscany, and are used in higher quantities to make the so-called Supertuscans.

The Tuscany wine of greatest stature is Brunello di Montalcino, a DOCG from a fortress town south of Sienna. The reds here are of legendary potency and a longevity that has commanded lofty prices.

Not far from Montalcino is Montepulciano, where you find the famous Vino Nobile. Similar to Chianti in composition, but fuller-bodied, Vino Nobile can stand among the finest wines in the world.

Carmignano merits special mention as a wine singled out for protection by the Grand Duke of Tuscany in 1716. Today this rare red made from Sangiovese and Cabernet has qualified as DOCG. But I doubt if it is widely known.

Tuscan whites rarely enjoyed much prestige in the past, probably because most of them were made of low-quality grapes except for Vernaccia di San Gimignano, which is made from the ancient Vernaccia vine. This is the only white DOCG wine.

Another famous white Tuscan is the fortified Vin Santo, which is pressed from semi-dried grapes and aged in small wooden

barrels. It is served as a dessert wine, and is especially delicious when accompanied with crisp Tuscan sweet biscuits called *cantuccini* or *biscotti*.

PIEDMONT

While five of the DOCG wines are from Tuscany, four are from Piedmont—thus reinstating the fact that these are two of the most important regions in Italy. Piedmont, in north-western Italy, is one of the country's richer regions. The four DOCGs from Piedmont are: Moscato d'Asti/Asti Spumante; Gattinara; Barbaresco; and, Barolo.

Whereas Tuscany is dominated by the Sangiovese grape, the major grapes of Piedmont are Barbera, Dolcetto, and Nebbiolo. Barbera and Dolcetto produce light styles of wine, and the Dolcetto is often compared with Beaujolais wines of France. From the Nebbiolo spring two of the greats of Piedmont, or rather of Italy: Barbaresco and Barolo.

Barbaresco, though made from the same Nebbiolo grape as Barolo, is generally lighter with less body than Barolo. Barbaresco must have a minimum alcohol level of 12.5 per cent, while Barolo must have 13 per cent. Barolo tends to be more complex than Barbaresco, because the latter needs to be aged for two years (one year in wood) to keep its DOCG status, while the former must be aged for at least three years (two in wood).

Another of Piedmont's DOCGs is Asti Spumante, a sparkling wine, for which Piedmont is well known. Sparkling wine in Italy is generally known by the name of either Spumante or Prosécco, while, as you know already, it goes by Champagne in France. Of course, not all French sparkling wine is Champagne, only the wine from that region, thus, Champagne is a regional name, while Prosécco, Italian sparkling wine, is actually the name of a grape.

The sparkling wine of Germany is called Sekt, which is neither a grape nor a region. In Spain, sparkling wine goes by the name cava. And surely there are other specific titles in other countries that produce it, but those mentioned here are the ones most widely known.

As for the best producers from Piedmont, if you buy wine from Gaja, Prunotto, or Renato Ratti, you will not go wrong.

VENETO

Veneto is one of Italy's largest wine-producing regions, situated in north-east, surrounding the glorious city of Venice. The name of the region is far less known than some of the wines that come from there: Valpolicella, Bardolino, and Soave. These are not great wines, but they are simple, tasty, easy-to-drink wines, and ready to consume young. Soave produces some of Italy's best white wines, but frankly, Italy is not well known for its whites.

OTHER REGIONS IN ITALY

Emilia and Romagna, the joint regions, as well as the gastronomic capital of Bologna, create wines that are affordable, easy to drink, and ideally suited to some of Italy's most delectable cooking. Emilia is the western sector, comprising the towns of Modena, Reggio, Parma, all cities associated with famous food products, like Modena's balsamic vinegar, or Parma's and Reggio's cheeses. The leading wine here is Lambrusco, which is a fizzy wine that is, oddly, dry in Italy, but often sweet when exported. I find that this wine goes very well with Indian food.

Other well-known wine regions in Italy include Umbria, home to the famous Orvieto, a rich white wine. As stated, Italy is not well known for its whites. But if you want to try a white from here, the best are Orvieto from Umbria, Soave from Piedmont, and Vernaccia di San Gimignano from Tuscany.

The Wines of
SPAIN

Spain is a world class producer of wines, both in quality and quantity. Better known are the quality reds from Rioja and Ribera del Duero, fine whites from Rueda, reds and whites from Penedés, the Sherry from Jerez, and a fine sparkling wine known as cava (primarily from Penedés, but made throughout Spain).

The wine industry in Spain is as old and established as that of France. Despite this similarity, the wines produced by these two countries are vastly different (possibly excepting certain wines from Rioja that are modelled on Bordeaux wines). Generally, Spain produces rather warmer style wines, which tend to be richer and higher in alcohol content than French wines. At the same time, Spain also makes plenty of sparkling wine and Sherry, a wine fortified with brandy, in a yeasty style peculiar to the country.

The wine classification of Spain is more or less just like the Italian system, so you will know enough about it by looking at the table later. As for the regions, I will mention those that are known around the world.

RIOJA

This is one of the best-known wine regions of Spain. Rioja wines originate in French know-how. The French taught the locals how to make wine from the local red Tempranillo grape variety. This is

a grape with a characteristic strawberry flavour, and makes smooth, velvety wines. Sometimes Garnacha, a red-wine grape from the Rhône (Grenache in French), is added. But the grape varieties are not mentioned in the labels of Rioja wines.

Spanish grapes and soil combined with French winemaking techniques resulted in the production of a series of red wines that are both very flavourful and strong. Enjoyed globally today, many of the Rioja reds are aged for ten years in large wooden barrels. This process gives these wines a distinct woody taste that many people find appealing.

There are also white Rioja wines, which are made from the lesser-known Viura grape (more widely known as Macabeo, and also used for cava). But the reds are surely the most popular, and are so rated: *Crianza*, the simplest, aged one year in oak barrels and one year in the bottle; *Riserva*, aged one year in oak barrels and two years in the bottle; and, *Gran Riserva*, aged two years in oak barrels and three years in the bottle.

Rioja wines are widely available in India, and the most dependable producer is the well-known Marques de Caceres.

RIBERA DEL DUERO

The Ribera del Duero (RdD) produces some of the best wines of Spain. The region, in the state of Castilla-Leon, runs along the Duero River for some 110 kilometres, though the best wines are centred around the province of Valladolid. Here the vines grow on chalky, pine-fringed slopes, the predominant variety being the Tinto Fino, which is a variant of the Rioja's Tempranillo. The legendary producer of the area is Vega Sicilia, but other bodegas (cellars or producers) of repute include Alejandro Fernandez and Perez Pascuas.

RUEDA

Rueda is a small region to the south-west of Valladolid, a separate delimited area from RdD, but also in Castilla-Leon. It is not very well known today, but the best whites from Spain are beginning to surface here, and thus it merits attention. The main grape varieties are the native Verdejo and the recently introduced Palomino, grown in calcareous clays. The district makes only white wines, for which it has had a local cult following since the seventeenth century. The newest wines are fresh and attractive, and will soon hit the world market in a big way.

PENEDÉS

Penedés is a region not too far from Barcelona. It is a huge area with over 25,000 hectares planted with vines, and is well known for good quality table wines, both red and white. The best known producer of the region is the Torres family. Penedés also specializes in the production of cava, or sparkling wines. This sparkling wine presents a good alternative to French Champagne and is often of very high quality. Currently consumers around the world are starting to drink more and more cava, and it is becoming quite popular.

The best-known cava are Codorniu and Freixenet, two of the biggest producers of bottle-fermented (that is, method champenoise) wines in the world. The two together control over 80 per cent of the cava industry in Spain. However, apart from the low price, the house brands of Codorniu and Freixenet are both on the lower side of mediocre. And considering that they are sold at pretty high prices in India—both of them are readily available here—it is hard to think of any reason to buy them.

SHERRY

Jerez is the Spanish word for what the English call Sherry. This city is one of the most famous of the Spanish wine regions. Sherry is perhaps what has made Spain's wine industry so famous. However, it was the British who made Sherry known worldwide in the nineteenth century. Sherry is still shipped to different parts of the globe from this city and is found in markets everywhere.

Indians perhaps know more about port, or porto, than Sherry. They are rather similar products, although a connoisseur of either would reject the comparison. Porto is, of course, a fortified wine from Portugal, which is a country that also produces wine, but these are not well known.

Sherry is a drink that deserves a book to itself, and should not be treated, or rather mistreated, in a wine book attempting to present an overview of world wines. Thus, we shall simply leave it at that.

Other
EUROPEAN WINES

The old world or European traditional wine-producing countries also include Austria, Portugal, Switzerland, Hungary, Bulgaria, and Greece, to name just the major exporters. On the whole, other than Austrian and Portuguese wines, the wines of the other countries mentioned are either quite good but too expensive (Hungary), quite inexpensive but not yet fully appreciated and/or regarded as too cheap (Bulgaria) or are quite bad and expensive (Switzerland) or quite bad and inexpensive (Greece). Austria makes good wines, but you could pretty much understand what they are all about if you have carefully read the section on German wines. The same goes for Portugal with respect to the Spanish section. Again, there is the divine Porto, but like Sherry, it deserves full attention devoted to it alone.

Any world wine guide should in fact contain sections on all the countries mentioned above, and should possibly even voyage out into Rumania, Croatia, and so on. But this is your complete wine guide for India, and the wines of the above-mentioned countries do not regularly make it to this market.

Other world wines do not have important classification systems, so I close this section with this table.

Classifications of
EUROPEAN WINES

	GERMANY	FRANCE	ITALY	SPAIN
Special Quality Wine	⁜ QmP	⁜ AOC	⁜ DOCG	⁜ DOC 0
Quality Wine	⁜ Qba	⁜ VDQS	⁜ DOC	⁜ DO
Regional Wine	⁜ Landwein	⁜ Vin de pays	⁜ IGT	⁜ Vino de Tirra
Basic Wine	⁜ Tafelwein	⁜ Vin de table	⁜ Vino da tavola	⁜ Vino de mesa

NON-EUROPEAN WINES

....

(New-World Wines)

The most widely known wine-producing countries which fall under the new world heading include the USA, Australia, South Africa, and Chile. There are plenty of others, just as there are many more countries creating fine wines in Europe than the four I mentioned. But basically, these are the only ones that need to be mentioned to fully understand the wine scene in India.

The Wines of
THE UNITED STATES OF AMERICA

International focus on American winemaking is entirely directed towards California. Nevertheless, wines are produced in 45 out of the 50 American states, and the wineries of New York and the Pacific Northwest produce some very fine, world-class wines. The cool climate in these areas allows its winemakers to copy the methods of their European counterparts with greater ease than California, which has a much warmer climate and a lot more sun than the famous European regions.

The wine industry is currently expanding in the state of Washington. White wines are the most successful, but some quality Merlots and Cabernets are also produced here. Washington grapes are high in quality and vineyards from Oregon use them to boost the flavour of their own wines, which are also now growing in recognition, at least in America.

Other wine-growing regions include the Finger Lakes area of New York, producing 6 per cent of the total US wines (California produces 90 per cent), and many German-style productions come out of the state of Michigan. You can even find wine made in the desert state of New Mexico and in potato states such as Idaho. But the most famous and most important region in America is surely California, and it is the only one you really need to be familiar with. I do not think we are going to see non-California American wines on the Indian market with any frequency.

CALIFORNIA

The west coast of the United States is a major producer of wine in the world market. Growing American interest in wine has helped the American wine industry to grow in great leaps during the past few decades, and now the United States is actually one of the largest producers of quality wines in the world.

American wine is trying to find a market in India, but its

already-high prices (before the Indian government slaps its outrageous 267+ per cent taxes on it) will continue to delay its entry. Turning Leaf and Carlo Rossi wines are the only ones widely available now, but only the former is worth trying. These big names originate from the California wine boom that began about 20 years ago.

As with much of American technology, the majority of new technologies used in winemaking were pioneered in California, and California wines win a surprising number of top awards in blind tastings around the world. Blind tasting means that one tastes and evaluates the quality of a wine without knowing anything about the wine's origin or technicalities. Since the wine-world had traditionally revolved around France, only French wines would win all the great awards, that is, until blind tasting came about, and permitted unbiased evaluations. It is in these unbiased evaluations where California wines really began to shine.

While the USA does not have a classification like most European countries, there is a consistent attempt to create something like it. Wines are regulated by the Bureau of Alcohol, Tobacco, and Firearms (BATF), which has pushed for some legal standards for labelling and production. This has taken the form of the AVA system, that is, American Viticultural Area. There are over 150 AVAs now, but there is still not a well-ordered manner of organizing and regulating them. However, some standards have been set, for example, a varietal wine must have at least 85 per cent of the grape variety mentioned on the label. Or, when a specific vineyard is mentioned on the label, 95 per cent of the grapes must have come from there. There are several other ways and means of regulating the industry, and one of these includes the legal determination of several terms of style that often appear on labels, such as 'Early Harvest' which is equivalent to German *Kabinett*, 'Late Harvest' which equals a German *Beerenauslese*, and 'Special Select Late Harvest' which is like German *TBA*. On the other hand, there is still no legal definition of the term 'Reserve' so, just as in India, it just might mean anything, or nothing, at all. Anyway, within California, there are several recognizable winemaking regions, which can be divided into three major groups: North Coast, Central Coast, and San Joaquin Valley.

North Coast:

The wines from the North Coast are the best and most widely known, as this region includes the counties of Napa, Sonoma, Mendocino, and Lake. The wines of California's Napa Valley are very popular and are especially competitive with the highest quality French wines.

Napa Valley uses about 80 per cent of its workable land for the cultivation of grapes. There are about 220 wineries in Napa with a total planting of 40,000 acres. The rich soil and balanced weather have proven perfect for quality grape growing. Wines from this region tend to be very big, very rich, and tannic. For the most part, the vineyards of Napa attempt to emulate French wines and have been successful in doing so. Within Napa are several famous 'micro-climates' such as Stag's Leap, and AVAs such as Carneros.

The Sonoma Valley is another important name for California winemaking. There are about 35,000 acres of vineyards controlled by around 175 wineries. Within Sonoma are some AVAs of good repute, Alexander Valley and Dry Creek are the two most famous. The wines of the producer Ridge are some of the finest California wines. Also, Stag's Leap from Napa is hard to beat.

Central Coast:

The Central Coast contains newer areas that are already showing great promise, all found in the counties of Monterey, Santa Clara and Livermore in the north, and San Luis Obispo and Santa Barbara in the south. One of the best producers in the Central Coast is Calera.

The Russian river valley is a rising star. Russian settlers way back in the olden days were the first to plant grapevines in this area, and lately the wines from these regions have begun to rival Napa Valley wines. The dense fog that passes through these areas result in the soft, fruity wines that the American public tends to favour.

San Joaquin Valley:

This is not a producer of fine wines, but it pumps out the greatest volume. Napa and Sonoma together only produce about 15 per cent of California wines, whereas the San Joaquin Valley makes about 55 per cent. The designation you are likely to encounter is Central Valley, which is in the San Joaquin Valley and should not be confused with the Central Coast. Central Valley wines are generally not as flavourful as those of Sonoma or Napa Valley. But since the wines from this area are much more affordable, the market for them continues to grow.

The Wines of
AUSTRALIA

Australia is a major and extraordinary producer of wines. It has produced world-famous wines for many years now, and an interesting fact is that the country now has the highest level of wine consumption among English-speaking countries. These countries tend to be beer drinking, and consider wine either snobbish or effete. But in Australia, everyone seems to enjoy drinking wine, and the snob factor has been entirely eliminated.

Like California, Australia benefits from experimenting with new technologies and unconventional methods of producing wine. Many people feel that the winemakers of Australia gain from having no strong tradition of winemaking, it has been a great experiment from the very start. The average Australian winemaker is said to mix blind enthusiasm with technical know-how, resulting in some of the most interesting and flavourful wines in the world.

Experimentation has led to unorthodox blends that are now legendary, such as Cabernet-Shiraz, something one would never find in the old world, but with results that even the French have to admit are astonishingly fine. The main grape varieties in Australia are, for reds, Shiraz (Syrah in France, used in the Rhône), Cabernet Sauvignon (used, of course, in Bordeaux), and Pinot Noir (used in Burgundy). The major whites are Riesling (resulting in very different wines from those of Germany), Semillon (in France, this is blended with Sauvignon Blanc to make white Bordeaux), and Chardonnay (used to make white Burgundy). I am pointing out the specific grapes used because Australia, as does all the new world, labels its wines by the grape type, in addition to mentioning the region.

Australia has around 30 distinct wine-growing regions, but only three of them are important for us: New South Wales; South Australia; and, Victoria.

NEW SOUTH WALES

Australia's New South Wales is one of its most successful wine regions. The Hunter Valley in this area grows about 60 different varieties of grapes. But the Valley gets very hot and grapes often rot before harvest. The wines of this valley are famous for their distinct taste that some describe as a 'sweaty saddle'. Hardly sounds appetizing, but if this gets Australian cowboys to drink wine, then there is no point in disputing it. Despite being famed for sweaty-saddle wines, the wines of the Hunter Valley are of very high quality and are sought after throughout the world, including France.

The best districts in New South Wales are Hunter Valley and Mudgee.

VICTORIA

During the nineteenth century, Victoria was the largest producer of wine in Australia. The Phylloxera outbreak that originated in the Americas and reached Europe in the 1850s, not only destroyed all the vineyards of the old world, but also struck Australia, and devastated the vineyards of Victoria, which did not really begin to recover until fifteen years back. Victoria has a very modern collection of grapes that are mixed with Bordeaux varieties, producing wines that are fragrant, with minty aromas. This wine industry is again growing and promises to be very important to the wine world within the next few years.

There are several districts in Victoria that turn out excellent wines: Bendigo, Geelong, Great Western, Goulburn Valley, Milawa, Moonambel, Mornington Peninsula, Rutherglew, and Yarra Valley.

SOUTH AUSTRALIA

About 60 per cent of Australia's wine is produced in South Australia. The red soil in the Coonawara region has a high mineral content that helps in the production of wines that are very rich in flavour and texture. A large number of Australia's most famous wines come from this area, and generally the highest quantity of wine for export is from South Australia.

Famous districts of South Australia include Adelaide Hills, Barossa Valley, Clare, Coonawarra, Padthaway, Southern Vales and McLaren Vale.

Penfolds is one of the best producers of wine in South Australia, but they also have a share in other districts. Indeed, most of Australia's top wineries produce wine in several districts – Rosemount Estate, for example, produces Hunter Valley wines, as well as South Eastern Australian varietals.

In addition to those already mentioned, Australia's best producers include: Brown Brothers, Lindemans, Orlando, Petaluma, Wolf Blass, Henschke, and Mountadam. Hardy's is a huge wine producer, operating in Australia a bit like Gallo does in the USA. Hardy's wines are widely available on the Indian market (more on them below), but they are not always very good examples of what Australia is capable of.

Australia has been watching the Indian import duties on wine, waiting, and strongly lobbying for them to be reduced. Australian wines will be one of the biggest competitors on the Indian scene as the Indian wine industry, and wine consumption, develops.

The Wines of
SOUTH AFRICA

The vines of Australia are all likely to have their original clippings brought from South Africa, back in the days when Australia was a huge British penal colony. South Africa has been producing wine ever since early Dutch colonial days, and its fine mixture of soil and climate make it an ideal place to cultivate the vine. One of the most famous vineyards, Groot Constantia, was planted back in 1684.

Vineyards are distributed throughout the country, but the leading ones are closer to Cape Town. Perhaps the best wines come from the Paarl Valley, in the Stellenbosch district, and around Wynberg. Interestingly, the great vineyards of South Africa are at about the exact same latitude south as the best vineyards of Chile and Australia.

Although South Africa has been producing wine since the seventeenth century, there has been little world-wide interest in its industry until recently (except a brief period of glory in the nineteenth century, where the wines were prized even in France). Because of international politics and economic policies, South Africa could hardly participate in the modern wine boom. Ever since these policies have changed, South African wines are starting to develop a following well beyond its borders.

The white wines of South Africa have a very good reputation in the international wine industry, being light, crisp and fruity. The Chenin Blanc and Chardonnay grapes, especially, seem to thrive in the South African climate. These grapes produce aromatic and spicy wines that compliment many different foods and tastes. I would think that the South African Chenin would go well with Indian food; the South African firm of Blouberg is selling wines in India. Indage also buys South African wines and bottles it in India.

Although the white wines of South Africa currently have a better international image than the reds, there are a number of very high quality red wines. One of the most flavourful South African red is a cross between the Pinot Noir and the Cinsault (a grape from southern Rhône). This wine is called Pinotage, and is exported around the world with great success.

South African Shiraz is another success. The wine is rich and heavy, with a high-alcohol content, and tends to have undertones, like all high-quality South African reds, of tobacco.

The Wines of
CHILE

Chilean wines are growing faster in popularity and recognition than any other wine industry in the world. Many tasters say that Chilean wine has a slightly peculiar taste that distinguishes it from more 'conventional' European wines, but I do not think that this is true, and I do not believe that this contention would hold up in blind tastings.

But you can decide for yourself about this, because Chilean wines have already hit Indian shelves. Indage imports Chilean wines and bottles and sells them under their own label, and Sula's now-famous Satori Merlot, as you already learned, is actually a Chilean wine in an Indian bottle.

The wine of this Latin country is earning a reputation as a product high in quality. This claim is worth investigating, especially since the cost per bottle remains comparatively very low.

Chile has a long history of producing wine, but only in the last decade has it become visible on the world market. Its climate is well suited for vines, and in fact the Chilean climate acts as a deterrent to the Phylloxera microorganism. In most of the world, the only solution to Phylloxera was to graft European grapevines onto American stocks, since the latter were not susceptible to Phylloxera. About 99 per cent of the vineyards in Europe today contain European vines (like Cabernet Sauvignon, Merlot, etc.) grafted onto American roots. American vines do not make quality wine, which is why the European ones must be used. Chile, however, is one of the only wine-producing regions in the world that does not have to graft its vines onto American roots. It can simply grow the whole European grapevine, roots and all, in its soil.

The chief wine region in Chile is the Maipo Valley. Here you find Chile's finest reds, but they have recently expanded the industry to produce high-quality whites as well. The Cabernet Sauvignon made in the Maipo Valley are world famous, and are characterized by a special smoky flavour.

Wineries such as Linderos, Concha y Toro and Undurraga produce some of the Maipo Valley's highest quality wines. The wines from these wineries are aged in large oak barrels and have a rich and complex flavour due to the barrel-ageing process.

Chile basically sells its wines with the grape variety clearly marked on the label. This appeals especially to the American market, but also to anyone who is horrified by the lack of the name of the grape variety on the labels of the most high-quality French wines. The major grape varieties produced in Chile are, for the reds, Cabernet Sauvignon, Merlot, and Syrah, and, for the whites, Chardonnay and Sauvignon Blanc.

WORLD WINES
AVAILABLE IN INDIA

WINES IMPORTED, BOTTLED, LABELLED AND/OR SOLD BY INDIA'S DOMESTIC PRODUCERS

The larger producers or firms (Indage, Sula, and Shaw Wallace) have a range of imported wines bottled in India, which often go by the name 'joint venture' wines, or something similar. Basically, these are wines imported in bulk, generally in huge tanks or vats, and then bottled and labelled in India in order to (1) reduce the duties paid on the imported wine, (2) permit the sale of the imported wine in certain regions where wine not bottled in India cannot be sold in shops (like Delhi), and (3) create a label that appeals specifically to the Indian market. Another nice thing about this method is that labour performed in India creates jobs here.

These joint venture wines are generally a bit more expensive than the Indian produced wines, although there is not much difference in price. Let us now run through these wines and evaluate them.

PLEASE CAREFULLY NOTE: In Part Three evaluations, I will not stick to the systematic three-step tasting notes. In the wines treated in Part Three, it is not necessary to guide the reader by the hand. There are far fewer risks involved in terms of acquiring a drinkable wine from the international market. All wines coming from the traditionally wine-producing countries are drinkable. So, there is only need of caution with respect to getting the best wine at the best price. Thus, the tasting notes will be less formal here than in Part Two. (The exception to this will be with joint venture wines, that is, any imported wine that is bottled in India, here, again, we need to be careful, and more precise.)

INDAGE WINES

Indage has the following eight joint venture wines, from Australia, South Africa, France, Germany, and Chile, currently available on the market:

1. Cranswick Indage Shiraz
2. Cranswick Indage Merlot
3. Cranswick Indage Chardonnay
4. Zulu Nelsons Creek Indage Pinotage
5. Taillan Indage Bordeaux
6. Peter Mertes Indage Rhine Pride Riesling
7. Morande Indage Sauvignon Blanc
8. Morande Indage Cabernet Sauvignon

AUSTRALIA

Cranswick is a well-known Australian winery, the biggest in western Australia, that has a few lines of varietal wines. My guess is that the joint venture Cranswick Indage wines (Shiraz, Merlot, and Chardonnay) use the wines from Cranswick's *Gnangara* series, which retail for about $9 in the USA. These wines, bottled in India, sell for Rs. 450 in Delhi, which is comparable to the US selling price—that makes this line of wines good value for us in India.

+++ CRANSWICK INDAGE SHIRAZ 2002

EYE: A rich, dark red.

NOSE: Nice nose, full of cherry with dashes of liquorice.

TASTE: This is a medium-bodied wine with only mild tannin, fruity with hints of chocolate.

EVALUATION

The wine usually sells for Rs. 490, making it a good buy. The wine is GOOD, but not worth over Rs. 500.

✣✣✣ CRANSWICK INDAGE MERLOT 2002

EYE: Deep ruby red.
NOSE: Bursts of raspberry and spice, and hints of rose.
TASTE: The alcohol (14 per cent) reigns supreme, but there are also fruity flavours, primarily cherry, and nice liquorice and chocolate touches.

EVALUATION
If you visit the Indage winery in Maharashtra, the wine is selling there for Rs. 455, making it a good buy. The wine is GOOD, but not worth over Rs. 475.

✣✣✣ CRANSWICK INDAGE CHARDONNAY 2002

EYE: Pale straw.
NOSE: Interesting, detectible guava.
TASTE: This is full of exotic flavours, but the acid, grapefruit and pineapple, is searing; there is some juicy mango that helps balance out the acid.

EVALUATION
At Indage itself, the wine sells for Rs. 455, making it a good buy. The wine is GOOD, but not worth over Rs. 475.

SOUTH AFRICA
The Zulu Nelson's Creek (Indage) Pinotage is produced by South Africa's middle-sized, family owned Nelson's Creek winery. Their Pinotage retails in the US for $7, so the bottled-in-India version that we get here for Rs. 450 is not a bad price.

✣✣/✣✣✣ ZULU NELSON'S CREEK INDAGE PINOTAGE 2002

With an alcohol level of 13.89 per cent, this is a heady wine.

EYE: The colour is ruby red.
NOSE: The nose is packed with red fruit and hints of violets.
TASTE: Primarily cherry flavour, with light tannin coating.

EVALUATION:
>   So heady and yet thin, Rs. 450 is pushing the limit.
>   The wine falls between AVERAGE and GOOD,
>   but is not worth more than Rs. 450.

FRANCE
✦✦✦ TAILLAN INDAGE, BORDEAUX 1999

Group Taillan is Bordeaux's largest shipper, and the city of Taillan is in Medoc. Since Taillan oversees the sale of so much wine, it is not possible to determine what the India bottled Taillan Indage Bordeaux actually is, or how it is sold in France itself. There is a very fine Chateau du Taillan, Haut Medoc, which is a traditional blend of 55 per cent Merlot, 35 per cent Cabernet Sauvignon, and 10 per cent Cabernet Franc, that sells for $10 a bottle in France and the USA, but I doubt that this is what we are getting here. There is also a **Taillan Merlot Vin de Pays d'Oc,** and this is more likely the base of the Taillan Indage Bordeaux on the Indian market. Normally, Rs. 470 is too much to pay for VDP d'Oc, which sell in France for around Rs. 60-120. But this wine is pretty decent, and beats many other wines on the market sold at this price.

EYE: Clear and bright, medium-hue red.
NOSE: Sawdust, some sulphur, some steel and then a
        good burst of Cabernet.
TASTE: Rather thin, but actually a pretty good balance,
        very mineral, salty even.

EVALUATION
>   The wine is getting old and worn out. The 1999
>   should no longer be on the market, but if you
>   can get your hands on any later vintage, buy it.
>   Even this one is GOOD for Rs. 470.

GERMANY
✦ PETER MERTES INDAGE RHINE PRIDE RIESLING

This is most likely not the Peter Mertes Riesling Classic, which is a well made white wine with nice acidity and citrus fruit. Rather, considering how thin and cloyingly sweet this Indage-bottled Rhine wine is, I presume it is not even a Qualitätswein. Whatever it is, Rs. 450 is an outrageous amount to ask for it.

EVALUATION
POOR.

CHILE

The Morande Indage Sauvignon Blanc and Cabernet Sauvignon are most likely the Morande *Pionero* range of varietal wines from Chile's Central Valley. These sell for about $9 in the USA, so Rs. 455 in India is a fair price.

✛ ## MORANDE INDAGE CABERNET SAUVIGNON 2000

EYE: Intensely red, sign of a hot climate, with a touch of purple.

NOSE: Cherry and toast, the fruit is not ripe, but it is generous, a touch sour.

TASTE: The sour touch in the nose comes through in the mouth, as does the toast—the toasty taste is lovely, the sourness is off-putting.

EVALUATION

A bit alcoholic, but certainly tasty with food. I think the 2000 vintage is two years past its prime. I also do not understand where the wine passed its time between 2000 and 2004, for the label shows that the wine was bottled in 2004. Was such a non-descript wine cellared in casks for so long? At Rs. 465, it is nothing more than AVERAGE.

✛ ## MORANDE INDAGE SAUVIGNON BLANC 2001

The Sauvignon Blanc fruit comes from the Curicó Valley, located in Chile's central zone. There are rich, alluvial soils in this region and this, in conjunction with a Mediterranean climate, makes it possible to produce grapes with a characteristic freshness.

EYE: Yellow gold, decent intensity.

NOSE: Lemon peel, butter, mandarin orange.

TASTE: Rich but flabby, lacking freshness, but nice orange finish.

EVALUATION
A bit alcoholic, but at Rs. 465, it is AVERAGE.

SULA VINEYARDS

SULA has two wines that are produced abroad and bottled/labelled in India, a white (Pacifica Chardonnay) and a red (Satori Merlot).

CALIFORNIA
++ PACIFICA CHARDONNAY

EYE: Green gold of decent intensity.
NOSE: Rather sour, a touch of butter suggestive of Chardonnay.
TASTE: Sweet and sour, some lemon.

EVALUATION
It could be my bottle, but the wine has a strange Chinese take-away quality about it. Uneven, imbalanced, but it will do. It is not cheap, though, so I cannot recommend it. AVERAGE.

CHILE
++ SATORI MERLOT

EYE: Satori has the sinister hue of a hot-climate red. Thus, it naturally has remarkably opulent legs.
NOSE: One is certainly first attacked by the sulphur, but shortly thereafter a drying whiff of woodiness, possibly grape stem, comes through. The bouquet is closed, however, so there is none of the berry one would hope for in a Merlot, but one senses that there will be plenty of tannin in the mouth.
TASTE: As second or third pressed as the colour makes the wine appear, the taste is remarkably sanitized, possibly a result of thorough filtration. There is a coating of what is probably stem tannin in the front of the mouth and cheeks, and finally a burst of Merlot wild berry character just at the finish. I also got a sense of vanilla, leading me to the notion that there is some oak involved, but I doubt my impression there.

Reflecting on the situation outside of India, I shudder at the thought that this wine costs $10 (Rs. 450)! It is without a doubt a $1 bottle of wine. But, alas, we are on, in and bound by the Indian market. And within this market, Satori Merlot is a decent buy for a simple wine to accompany food at the table. One must wonder, however, why Sula selected such a low-quality wine from Chile, when the country makes so many wonderful bargain wines. Could not they have chosen something better even at the same price? AVERAGE.

SHAW WALLACE

FRANCE

Shaw Wallace is about to begin importing a line of French wines called Papillion in bulk to bottle them in India. There will be a red, white, and a sparkling wine. They have yet to work out the logistics, so it is not sure when they will appear on the market.

INTERNATIONAL BOTTLED-IN-ORIGIN WINES DISTRIBUTED BY DOMESTIC PRODUCERS

A second group of international wines available on the Indian market (the first being the joint ventures discussed above) is the collection of wines imported and distributed by domestic Indian producers. At present, the only major players in this are Shaw Wallace and Sula. The latter has a range called Sula Selections. The wines of these two companies are simply bottled-in-origin wines from various regions around the world, which the domestic producers have decided to import and distribute. These include

wines from the USA, France, Spain, Argentina, Australia, Chile, Italy, and South Africa. Neither Sula nor Shaw Wallace is sole distributor of all of these wines, however, so there would be some overlap of this section with the next category of international wines on the Indian market, that is, those imported/distributed by the international companies themselves, such as E.J. Gallo. First, we will evaluate the Sula Selections, then we will move on to the wines distributed by Shaw Wallace, and then, finally, we will end Part Three by covering those wines imported by the international companies themselves.

NOTE REGARDING EVALUATION OF THESE WINES:
The bottled-in-origin wines sell in many different venues in India, retail shops, restaurants, hotels, wine bars, etc. They will, therefore, sell at very different prices not only state by state, but also venue by venue. Furthermore, all of the wines are at the least GOOD wines, unless otherwise noted. As for vintage, wines listed without a particular year are described in their general character (how the wine tends to be year after year). Thus, the most helpful rating for the consumer, I believe, would be to evaluate these wines by giving the maximum price you should pay in a retail setting. Obviously, you can expect to pay double or even triple at a restaurant, but that's another story. In short, my evaluation of each wine will tell you how much the wine is worth. So, if you are finding it for more in the market, then you are paying too much.

SULA SELECTIONS

FRANCE

I   FORTANT DE FRANCE
The Fortant label is the recognized leader in varietal wines from France's Midi region.

a)	Fortant Sauvignon Blanc

The Sauvignon Blanc has a full bouquet with a good balance of fruit and freshness. The full bouquet is matched by the richness in the mouth.

EVALUATION
Fortant are good-value bargain wines outside of India, costing $7 in the USA. It would be absurd, however, to pay more than Rs. 490 for a bottle.

b)	Fortant Vin De Pays d'Oc Chardonnay

The robe is pale gold. The bouquet gives hints of ripe citrus fruit. These are confirmed on a very smooth palate along with attractive peach flavours and a clean finish.

EVALUATION
Same as Fortant Sauvignon Blanc.

c)	Fortant Vin De Pays d'OC Cabernet Sauvignon

This is a light, easy-to-drink Cab with good balance. It has berry and black currant flavours and a smooth finish.

EVALUATION
Same as Fortant Sauvignon Blanc.

d)	Fortant Vin De Pays d'OC Merlot
This Merlot has a gentle fruity aroma, is soft yet full-bodied and very easy on the palate.

EVALUATION
Same as Fortant Sauvignon Blanc.

e)	Fortant Vin De Pays d'OC Syrah

This 100 per cent Syrah is a dark red, heady wine with sweet black fruit and a touch of liquorice.

EVALUATION
Same as Fortant Sauvignon Blanc.

II	MICHEL LYNCH
Michel Lynch was a Frenchman of Irish descent who became Mayor of Bordeaux just before the 1789

Revolution. He is said to be famed for throwing the keys of the guillotine to the revolutionaries.

a) Michel Lynch Bordeaux Blanc
This is a blend of Sauvignon and Semillon. It is a pale lemon-gold, with a bouquet of gooseberry and green apples. The wine is dry and firm with a crisp acidity.

EVALUATION
It is a lovely wine, selling for $15 (Rs. 700) in the USA. It would be unwise to spend more than Rs. 850 for it.

b) Michel Lynch Bordeaux Rouge

This is a consistent, nice, basic minor Bordeaux. The addition of Merlot to Cabernet Sauvignon brings softness to the wine and makes it ready to drink within two or three years. It has a gentle bouquet, is firm and middleweight on the palate with a pleasant dry finish.

EVALUATION
This sells cheaply outside of India ($7), and I would not dream of paying more than Rs. 500 for it.

III CHAMPAGNE TAITTINGER

a) Taittinger Brut Réserve

The Taittinger Champagne house has a reputation as one of the finest Grandes Marques, or major labels. Their Brut Reserve is elegant, delicate, heavily Chardonnay influenced, and has a unique flowery perfume.

EVALUATION
Champagne is always expensive. You can buy this at the duty free shop for $27, and it is easily worth it. A good price in India would be Rs. 1600.

b) Comtes de Champagne Blanc de Blancs 1995

This is made exclusively from Chardonnay. It is an extraordinary wine! The 1995 displays aromas of damp brioche followed by flavours of crisp orange marmalade, mineral, with a long elegant finish, earthy and complex.

EVALUATION

> One does not get the chance to taste something like this very often. It will set you back around $170 in the duty free shop. It should sell for something like Rs. 10,000 in India.

c)   Comtes De Champagne Rose 1996

This extraordinary Champagne is a blend of 70 per cent Pinot Noir and 30 per cent Chardonnay, where only the free run juice is used. The robe is amber rose with numerous very fine bubbles. The bouquet is full of strong fruit, jam, and forest berries. It is very vibrant and alive in the mouth, with cherry flavours, very ample. The wine is bottle-aged for five years before being released in the market.

EVALUATION

> A great bubbly for a special anniversary. Do not pay more than Rs. 3,000 for it, though.

⊹

SPAIN

I.   MARQUES DE CACERES

The Marqués de Cáceres winery was founded by Enrique Forner in 1970. As owner of the Bordeaux Grand Cru Classé Chateau Camensac, Forner brought Bordeaux experience to Rioja. The winery has been guided by the policy of steering away from heavy oak characteristics towards wine that still uses oak, but also gives rich, fruity, supple flavours with intense aromas.

a)   Marques de Caceres Red

The label states 'Vendimia Seleccionada', which literally means that the vintage has been selected, but its significance is that this is a Crianza wine, that is, one with limited oak ageing compared to Reserva or Gran Reserva. The usual blend is 85 per cent Tempranillo with the addition of Graciano and Garnacha (Grenache). It is aged in small oak barrels for 16 months. It has a bright ruby colour with hints of vanilla on the bouquet before displaying raspberries on the palate, with a slight touch of pepper.

EVALUATION

> I love this wine. In Europe, where it is good value at $13, one can drink it often. In India, I would perhaps, pay up to Rs. 1,000.

b)   Marques De Cáceres White

This crisply acidic, lovely, fresh white wine is made exclusively from the Viura grape. It has soft flavours of melon and citrus/floral, and hints of tart lemon and orange blossom.

EVALUATION

> This does not match the red by any means, but it is a nice alternative to the more commonly found varietals. The top price would be Rs. 650.

✣

ARGENTINA

The wines of Argentina were not covered in the general overview above. It is a rising star, but not nearly as significant as the countries focussed upon. Actually, Argentina is the largest wine producing and wine consuming country of the Western hemisphere, but it exports hardly anything—the people drink it all themselves. The vast majority of Argentine wine is basic, not fine. The finer wines, which are the ones that you are likely to encounter, such as the Trapiche discussed below, are from the Mendoza region. Another region known for better production is San Juan, but there are no wines from there currently available in India. The vineyards are planted along the foothills of the Andes, not far from the Chilean border.

I   TRAPICHE, MENDOZA, ARGENTINA

a)   Astica Sauvignon Blanc-Semillon (12.5%) 2003

This is a blend of 60 per cent Semillon with 40 per cent Sauvignon Blanc. It is an elegant dry white wine, with a gold robe tinged with green, very fresh with light notes of vanilla. The aroma is full of citrus fruit.

EVALUATION

> This is the best of the Astica line, selling for about $8 in the USA. In India, I might pay Rs. 600 for it.

b)   Astica Torrontes (13%) 2003

This is a grape that comes from Galicia in Spain and is used also in the Rioja. It is sometimes used along with Viura to make good quality white Rioja wines. It is fascinating that Argentina should be creating varietals from the grape, and the results are certainly not bad. This wine has a highly aromatic nose with Muscat and honeysuckle being prominent. The acid is crisp and the wine as a whole is light and pleasant.

EVALUATION

This is an interesting wine, unquestionably. It sells for $7 in the USA. I would pay Rs. 550 for it, just for a change.

c)   Astica Tempranillo (13%) 2003

This 100 per cent Tempranillo wine is a dark, rich red like the wines of Rioja. One can taste cherries and berry fruit, and there is a nice suggestion of vanilla in the nose.

EVALUATION

This is a cheap wine, costing around Rs. 225 in the USA. To pay more than Rs. 450 would be a crime.

d)   Astica Merlot-Malbec (13%) 2003

This light red (50 per cent Merlot and 50 per cent Malbec) is nicely aromatic, though alcohol does dominate the nose. It is nice and dry with soft tannin.

EVALUATION

Indage's IVY Malbec costs Rs. 450, and it is just as good as this one.

AUSTRALIA

I   HARDY'S

a)   Nottage Hill Chardonnay (12.5%) 2001

Hardy's Nottage Hill wines are lively and fruit-driven. Nottage Hill lies just outside the village of McLaren Vale, in

South Australia. The place is named after Tom Nottage, nephew of Thomas Hardy, the company's founder. According to Hardy, this wine is produced from fully-ripened fruit and machine-harvested during the cool of the night. In order to retain the freshness, it is cold fermented in stainless steel tanks and undergone partial malolactic fermentation. Following blending and oak maturation, the wines are stored in stainless steel tanks to maintain freshness prior to bottling. The wine is full-bodied with ripe tropical fruit flavours with butterscotch and oak complexity.

EVALUATION

> This is a lovely wine, costing $10 in the USA. I suppose I would pay as much as Rs. 800 for it in India.

b) Hardy Stamp Series

The Stamp range is identified by an original Australian postage stamp, dating back to 1937, which is featured on all Stamp of Australia wines. I love this series of wines, because they are not only cheap but also of very good quality. In India, however, they are not cheap, thus making it difficult for me to recommend them here.

c) Stamp of Australia Chardonnay Semillon (12.5%) 2001

Medium straw in colour, the wine displays aromas of peach, melon and lime. A creamy mouth feel, a fresh lime finish, and a subtle oak influence completes this medium-bodied wine.

EVALUATION

> The Stamp series cost $5 each in the USA (Rs. 250), and I drink them very often there. In India, they are selling for somthing in between Rs. 570-750. The latter price is absurd; I am comfortable paying Rs. 570, especially for the Shiraz-Cabernet.

d) Stamp of Australa Riesling-Gewurztraminer (12.5%) 2001

Medium straw in colour, this Riesling-Gewurztraminer shows fresh, floral fruit aromas with a touch of spice. The palate is full of tropical fruit and lychee.

EVALUATION

> Same as Chardonnay Semillon.

e)   Stamp of Australia Cabernet-Merlot (12.5%) 2001

Ruby red with purple hues, the Cabernet-Merlot offers aromas of blackcurrants, cherries, and plums.

EVALUATION
> Same as Chardonnay Semillon.

f)   Stamp of Australia Shiraz-Cabernet (12.5%) 2001

The blend marries the unique characteristics of two classic varieties. The spicy pepper, raspberry, and cherry fruit flavours of the Shiraz complements the capsicum, mint, and blackcurrant characters of the Cabernet Sauvignon. The wine is lightly oaked, so the fruit and flavours of the two varieties dominate.

EVALUATION
> Same as Chardonnay Semillon.

CHILE

I   SANTA RITA

a)   120 Merlot (13%) 2001

Chile produces some very good wine, easy on the wallet. Medium ruby. Nose is pleasant, largely black-currant, and other black fruits. When first opened it is a bit astringent, but after breathing it transforms into a jammy mix of blackcurrant and blackberry. Dry, but the ample fruit keeps it from being austere.

EVALUATION
> This costs $6 in the USA (Rs. 275). In India, I would not pay more than Rs. 570.

b)   120 Chardonnay (14.1%) 2000

This is from the Maipo Valley. It is a brilliant yellow-green, of medium intensity. Citric aroma with butter and vanilla notes. To the palate it is a fresh, tasty, and nicely persistent wine. It is oak aged and left on its lees after fermentation.

EVALUATION

> I suppose I would go as high as Rs. 650, if I were very thirsty for Chardonnay, which is not easy to find in India.

✣

ITALY

I   RUFFINO
ORVIETO CLASSICO SECCO, DOC

Dry and pleasant, easy to drink before and with dinner.

EVALUATION

> This is not a great wine, but I would go as high as Rs. 650.

II   LIBAIO CHARDONNAY, TOSCANA, IGT

Clean, crisp style. Bright, fresh and fruity, with pineapple, apple and apricot character. Medium-bodied, with good acidity. It is a blend of 90 per cent Chardonnay and 10 per cent Pinot Grigio.

EVALUATION

> Be warned, this wine neither travels nor ages well. I have had a terrible experience with it. If you dare to try it, do not pay more than Rs. 650.

III   AZIANO CHIANTI CLASSICO, DOCG 2001

Lighter than some in its class, but nice, with integrated spice, currant-cherry, mineral flavours. Youthfully tannic, a bit dry and tart now.

EVALUATION

> A nice, rich wine. I might pay up to Rs. 900 for it.

IV   CHIANTI CLASSICO RISERVA DUCALE, DOCG 2000

It is typical Chianti, especially in the nose: light, earthy berry. Good dried cherry and dried mushroom character, with medium body, delicate tannin.

EVALUATION

This wine is legendary, but overpriced. Do not go over Rs. 1200.

V CHIANTI RUFFINO, DOCG

Pale, ruby red. Another classic Chianti, with floral hints, especially violets. Well-balanced.

EVALUATION

This is a basic wine from Ruffino. It should not sell for more than Rs. 500. I would not pay a paisa more than Rs. 550.

VI MODUS, IGT

Lots of new wood yet rich and fruity, with loads of plum, toasty oak, and meat character. Full-bodied, soft and round, with a long finish. A blend of Sangiovese, Cabernet Sauvignon, and Merlot. This is a great Supertuscan.

EVALUATION

This will fetch as much as Rs. 2500.

VII TENUTA GREPPONE MAZZI, BRUNELLO DE MONTALCINO, DOCG

Brunellos are big wines, and this one is typical, with blackberry jam and smoky oak. The body is full but the tannin are soft and round.

EVALUATION

You could find yourself shelling out around Rs. 3;250 for this. If you have that sort of money to burn, then try the wine—it is wonderful.

SOUTH AFRICA

I J.C. LE ROUX LE DOMAINE (7.5%) NON-VINTAGE

This is a blend of Sauvignon Blanc and Muscadel. The juices of the two wines are kept separate before being transferred to steel tanks. Cold fermentation is initiated and lasts 21 days. The wine is blended in an average ratio of 80 per cent Sauvignon Blanc to 20 per cent Muscadel. Thereafter, the wine is carbonated and matured for three months in the bottle before release. The wine is a bright, green-yellow and sparkling with a bubbling Muscat aroma supported by fruit on the nose. The palate is sweet tropical fruit.

EVALUATION

It costs $5 in the USA, and that is, perhaps, $2 too much. Here, for more than twice that amount, it is not possible to recommend: POOR.

11   TWO OCEANS

A series by Distell, South Africa's largest producer of wine. In a way, it is South Africa's answer to E.J. Gallo of the USA or Hardy's of Australia.

a)   Two Oceans Chardonnay (13%) 2001

Winemaker Kobus Gerber describes this as a medium-bodied wine, light straw in colour with a tinge of green. It shows an abundance of citrus aromas and tastes supported by vanilla oak flavours. This Distell label takes its name from the two great oceans that converge at the Cape, the Indian, and the Atlantic. Grapes for this wine were sourced from Stellenbosch, Malmesbury, and Robertson. The juice received no skin contact. Fermentation in stainless steel tanks took place at 12°C. After which 40 per cent was transferred into a combination of second and third-fill 300 litre French oak barrels, where it spent six months and was stirred on the lees every second week. No malolactic fermentation was induced.

EVALUATION

I have heard these are selling for Rs. 555. Buy it at that price!

b)   Two Oceans Sauvignon Blanc (13%) 2000

The grapes came from vineyards in the Stellenbosch and Durbanville. The vines were established in deep Clovelly and Hutton soils rich in decomposed granite. In the cellar the juice received four hours skin contact and was fermented cold at 12-14°C for 14-21 days. Tropical nuances on the nose with subtle guava and fresh grass aromas. On the palate it has a firm and crisp entry and asserts the fruitiness found on the nose. It is finely structured and well-balanced with typical herbaceous undertones and discreet shades of ripe gooseberry and guava. About the 2001 (12.4 per cent alcohol), winemaker Karl Lambour says this is an elegant wine with ripe, gooseberry flavours backed by green fig and guava and a long, yet crisp, finish. About the 2003 (11.7 per cent alcohol), winemaker Thinus Engelbrecht says this is an elegant but crisp wine with ripe, gooseberry flavours on the fore palate backed by tropical fruits and a hint of grassiness that lingers long on the aftertaste.

EVALUATION

Same as Two Oceans Chardonnay.

c) Two Oceans Pinotage (14%) 2000

On the nose the wine has intense varietal aromas of baked banana, ripe strawberries, and stewed fruit. On the palate it is medium-bodied with red berry flavours and subtle tannin coupled to an elegant spicy finish. About the 2001 (14.4 per cent alcohol), winemaker Coenie Snyman says the wine shows red plum colours tinged with cerise. On the nose it elicits aromas of plum fruit backed by spicy vanilla, and on the palate it is medium-bodied with a distinctive berry fruit aftertaste. The wine was fermented for four days on the skins to preserve as much colour and fruit as possible. The wine was matured on French oak staves for nine months.

EVALUATION

Same as Two Oceans Chardonnay.

d) Two Oceans Shiraz (13.07%) 2001

Grapes for the Shiraz were sourced from both bush and trellised vineyards in Stellenbosch, Paarl, Malmesbury and Worcester. The wine was fermented for four days on the skins to preserve as much colour and fruit as possible. The wine was matured on French oak staves for nine months. Winemaker Coenie Snyman describes the wine as having lively ruby red colour. On the nose it gives aromas of red berry fruit and spices, while on the palate it reveals ripe fruit backed by soft easy tannin. He says this medium-bodied wine can be enjoyed now, but will improve with further maturation. About the 2002 (13.8%), winemaker Thinus Kruger describes this wine as deep ruby red in colour with fruit, spices and black pepper on the nose. It is medium-bodied with a slight tannic backbone and lots of ripe fruit.

EVALUATION
> Same as Two Oceans Chardonnay.

SHAW WALLACE SELECTIONS

FRANCE

I. CORDIER OF BORDEAUX

a) Cordier Bordeaux White (Sec.)

This is a crisp dry white made from Sauvignon Blanc, with a nice mineral-rich character.

EVALUATION
> I have generally found this wine overpriced. It sells for $9 in the USA, and I would not pay more for it here. Let us say it is worth Rs. 500.

b) Cordier Bordeaux Red

This simple but clean red is a blend of 45 per cent Cabernet Sauvignon and 55 per cent Merlot. The Merlot dominates, giving cherry flavours, while the Cabernet provides tannic structure. It is easy to drink and enjoyable.

EVALUATION
> It is a decent wine, selling for $10 in the USA. I might go as high as Rs. 700 here.

c) Cordier Saint-Emilion Red

The Saint-Emilion is more rich and tannic than the simpler Bordeaux red. It is a deep garnet, lightly oaked wine with strong suggestions of prune.

EVALUATION
> This is costly in the USA, selling at $20. The trick with this is that the wine should be well handled

and stored. If it is, I might pay as much as Rs. 1200, on a birthday.

II   LANSON OF CHAMPAGNE
LANSON BLACK LABEL BRUT

Lanson's Black Label Brut is a house-style Champagne of high quality, which is cellar-aged for three years before release. It is a blend of 35 per cent Chardonnay, 50 per cent Pinot Noir, and 15 per cent Meunier. Lanson, unlike most Champagnes, does not permit the wine to undergo malolactic fermentation, in order to try to generate a fresher style—the wine is characterized by toast and honey.

EVALUATION
You can buy this for $32 at the Duty Free shop. I am not sure it is worth it, considering the alternatives. I would not pay more than Rs. 1700 for it.

III   DUC DE VENTADIS
DUC DE VENTADIS VIN MOUSSEUX BRUT

This vin mousseux, or sparkling wine, is very little known around the world, and I have not had a chance to taste it. I am somewhat suspicious of the label.

EVALUATION
Try it if you want, but I am steering clear of it.

ITALY

I   FOLONARI OF THE VENETO

Folonari is produced by the largest wine company in Italy. Shaw Wallace has brought in three basic Folonari wines that are light, fresh, and match with many Indian dishes.

a)   Folonari Valpolicella

Dry, fresh fruity red wine with cherry flavours. It can be served slightly chilled, and drunk with anything. It is a very simple wine.

EVALUATION
The Folonari label sells for $7 in the USA. It is

not worth more. I would not pay anything more than Rs. 475 for it.

b)   Folonari Bardolino

Bardolino is similar to Valpolicella, with the vineyards some 10 kilometres away, although the soil there is very different. It never produces great wines, but the best of them are fresh and delightful, usually not much darker than a rosé wine. They tend to be low in alcohol. This is a very simple wine.

EVALUATION
Same as Folonari Valpolicella.

c)   Folonari Soave

One of Italy's best regions for white wines, though at the same time, not complicated whites like those of Burgundy, but simple, fresh, soft, light, drinkable wines good for any occasion.

EVALUATION
Same as Folonari Valpolicella.

THE UNITED STATES OF AMERICA

I   PAUL MASSON OF CALIFORNIA

Paul Masson sells tons and tons of wine, especially in America, but only a small amount is sold abroad (primarily to countries that do not produce wine). Their simple lines are sold in re-sealable carafes rather than standard bottles, and this makes them good for casual occasions like camping or picnics.

a)   Paul Masson White Wine

This is actually called California Chablis, which is an outmoded practice of calling non-French wines by French names—thus was Champagne used for every sort of sparkling wine outside of France, until the French managed to lobby hard enough to have it stopped. Most international firms gave up this label piggy-backing, but Paul Masson insists on calling its cheap jug white after one of France's most prestigious white wine regions.

EVALUATION
> The wine is as cheap as it can be (it sells for just a couple of dollars in the US) and does not merit much attention.

b)   Paul Masson Red Wine

Again, this does not merit much attention. It is the simplest of jug wines, and its only virtue outside of India is that it is dirt cheap and comes in re-sealable carafes that can later be used for other things. In India, however, it is not cheap, and thus I cannot recommend it for any reason.

EVALUATION
> Same as white above.

II   ARBOR MIST, NEW YORK

Arbor Mist wines are varietal wines injected with fruit additives. They are beastly abominations, something along the lines of the teenager's wine cooler, although a bit more defensible due to the existence of authentic fruit-laced wines like Spanish Sangria.

a)   Arbor Mist Blackberry Merlot

Obviously, whether Merlot or Bangalore Purple, when a varietal wine is adulterated, it is not possible to judge the quality of the original. There is no point in evaluating this wine. I will mention, however, just for comparison, that these sell for $7 per 1.5 litres, $4 per .75l, and $2.50 per .325l bottles in the USA. They are not worth anything more.

b)   Arbor Mist White Zinfandel (%)

See: Black berry Merlot (above)

WORLD WINES WIDELY AVAILABLE IN INDIA

(World Wines Imported by the International Company)

In Part Three we have already discussed and evaluated about 50 different wines currently on the Indian market. These have all been imported, international wines, whether they were imported in bulk and bottled in India, or were bottled-in-origin wines imported by domestic manufacturers. Although 50 wines is a pretty big number, there are about five times this number of international wines currently on the Indian market!

We cannot evaluate every single one of them here, but we have covered those that show up most frequently. If you encounter any wine we have not treated, then you will find general information about it from the first section of Part Three, the overview of world wines. Through the information there, you can track down the origin of your wine and get a grasp of its basic character. Wed this theoretical knowledge to your actual experience of the wine, and you will have mastered yet another label.

In the final section, the most prevalent wines on the market that have not yet been covered are discussed. There are basically four major producers/importers, and you will see their wines all over the place. These are Barton & Guestier and Georges Duboeuf of France, E. & J. Gallo of the USA, and Henkell of Germany. Two of them (B&G and Gallo) are huge producers that flood the global market with their mediocre wines. I do not like the majority of products from any of these producers/importers. But it is necessary to describe a bit of what each of them sell in India, so that the consumers have an idea of the choices they have before them. We will begin with the smallest, Henkell, and move to the largest, Gallo.

HENKELL (GERMANY)

Henkell is a well-known producer of Sekt or German sparkling wine, and they also import Riesling wines into India. For a full understanding of German Rieslings, review the section on German wines at the beginning of Part Three. As Riesling is a grape that will not grow well in most parts of India (there is some hope for it in Himachal Pradesh), it is advisable to experiment with any of the German Rieslings that you may come across in India. But be forewarned, go for the drier wines, or those labelled Trocken.

A popular wine in India is Henkell Trocken, which is Sekt, or sparkling wine. It is a decent example of generic German Sekt, and tends to be well priced. It should not cost you more than Rs. 600 for a 750 ml bottle, and the much more festive magnum bottles (1.5 l) should not cost more than Rs. 1300. Incidentally, in Germany, the magnum is available for about $13 or Rs. 600.

GEORGES DUBOEUF (FRANCE)

Duboeuf is legendary for having forced a pretty inferior wine (Beaujolais nouveau, aka. Beaujolais primeur) into every single wine shop in Europe and America. He turned the production of cheap wine into a media event, and now each year people from around the world flock to Beaujolais in order to watch the cars race out packed with cartons of nouveau wine to be distributed to the global bourgeoisie.

Duboeuf is a great marketing company and distributor and a mediocre quality overseer. They are a *negociant,* or bottlers/traders of wine. There are numerous labels under their wing, and most of the Beaujolais you find in India will be from Duboeuf.

Duboeuf sells one excellent wine, and the rest hover around lower or higher sides of mediocre. The best is the Fleurie, which is the most expensive of the *crus* of Beaujolais and probably also the best the region has to offer. The wines of Fleurie are fresh, floral, and fragrant, made with the Gamay grape, as are all Beaujolais wines, the Fleurie is one of the few wines from the region that age beautifully.

Notice that Duboeuf's Fleurie sells in the West for no more than $20, or Rs. 1,000. This is the only one of Duboeuf's wines that is worth the price in India.

BARTON & GUESTIER (FRANCE)

Known as B&G, this French powerhouse has been around for over 275 years. In the 1950s, B&G linked up with Seagram, a company (now known as Diageo) with a huge presence not only in India but everywhere. B&G, thus, is part of the mega company Diageo, and have all the might and market of Seagram to ride on. And what does all this power and capital do for us in India? Not much. B&G supplies a line of decent, but totally unexciting wines, the best of which are far too expensive, and the affordable of which are not good enough to buy.

First come a line of Private Selection Vin de Pays d'Oc. These are a range of varietal wines from southern France: Cabernet Sauvignon, Chardonnay, Merlot, Merlot-Shiraz, Sauvignon Blanc, and Shiraz. How are they? Great for the $4 (Rs. 200) they sell for in France. In India, it would be a crime to pay more than double for them.

Then they have the Gold Label series AOCs. These include a couple of decent Beaujolais Villages wines and a good, cheap Chateauneuf-du-Pape. The Pape costs $12 in France, $15 in the USA, so do not pay more than Rs. 825 for it.

B&G have a great many other wines, but I think I have prepared you well enough for them in the first section of Part Three. Again, being a part of Seagram, B&G will pop up everywhere. Their wines are worth trying only if the prices are right.

E. & J. GALLO (U.S.A)

Earnest and Julio Gallo is the world's biggest winery. This California winery alone makes more wine than the entire country of Australia! The vast majority of this wine is cheap plonk, and is sold under various names such as Bartles and James, Carlo Rossi, and so on. Please, do not buy Carlo Rossi—it is California's version of Bosca.

Gallo sold over 3,000 cases of wine in India in the year 2003-04. That makes Gallo India's largest importer. Gallo wine is quite good at the usual price of $5 a bottle (Rs. 250); but not so for the prices they fetch in India, which is as much as double the normal price. This is for the Wine Cellars (aka Sierra Valley) wines, not the more expensive and superior single vineyard wines like Frei Cabernet.

Indeed, Gallo has some excellent wines like the Frei Cabernet mentioned and Stefani Chardonnay, and so on. However, the Gallo line that they push in India is the Wine Cellars/Sierra Valley, low-priced wines (low-priced outside of India, that is).

Gallo has so many wines in so many countries that it is hard to keep track of which names they use where. We know that Wine Cellars is the same as Sierra Valley, even though both can be found on the Indian market. What is not clear is how the Turning Leaf label might show up here.

Under the Wine Cellars/Sierra Valley label are a number of noble varietals, and a handful of cheapies like Ruby Cabernet and White Zinfandel. The nobles include Cabernet Sauvignon, Chardonnay, Merlot and Zinfandel. All of the Wine Cellars/Sierra Valley label are probably to be avoided, unless you can get them for Rs. 350 or under.

Turning Leaf is another story. Some of these wines can be good value, especially the Cabernet Sauvignon and the Zinfandel. Turning Leaf also includes a Chardonnay, Sauvignon Blanc, and a Merlot. This range sells in the USA for about $7 (Rs. 350), and I think I would even go up to Rs. 550 for them.

EPILOGUE

You have just been introduced to a whole world of wines. In India and also in most of the West, wine seems still to be equivalent to French wine. The majority of all the imported wine sold in India is French, and there is no indication that this trend will change soon. But the world of wine continues to expand. Alongside the famous Bordeaux and Burgundy, you will also find German and Italian wines served at posh formal dinner parties in Europe and in America. You might also see California wines as well as Australian, Chilean, and South African on the table.

As the Indian market develops, I foresee a time in the future when you might even find a fine Indian wine being served in top New York restaurants. But the time between then and now will have to encompass a great many changes.

First, Indians need to become much more wine savvy. Until the Indian consumer knows what he or she wants from a wine, local producers will follow the age-old rules of capitalism, and make the lowest quality product that they can get away with. You must help to keep Indian winemakers from trying to get away with selling abhorrent plonk in a prettily-labelled wine bottle.

As it stands, much of the affordable imported wine on the Indian market right now is also of a relatively low quality. We cannot blame the foreign companies, but rather the Indian regulations on the importation of wine.

Secondly, the Indian import scheme has to change in order to let winemakers bring in a decent product. Currently, a bottle of wine that would cost $1 in France would cost, after Indian taxing (and not including shipping costs), about $4. That is a precious Rs. 200 for a wine that the French would pour down the drain.

A wine that the average Frenchman would drink with his meal, costing, say, $2.50, would cost a hefty Rs. 350 in India—inclusive of taxes but not shipping cost. This, too, would be sales without profit for the winemaker, even though I guess the Indian government makes a good profit at the expense of both the importer and buyer.

For some reason, the 5-star hotels are free from paying this duty. It is the retailers who should be given a break, so that the consumers can get wines worth drinking at reasonable prices. The government wants to prevent this in order to let the domestic industry have a chance to get a foothold so it can compete when the imports flood the market.

Indage did not try to make anything decent until it got a jolt from Sula. And yet, Sula itself has not really tried to make wine as much as they have tried to make money. Grover, then, another classic Indian company, has only just started to work to improve their wines. Only since 2002 has anything worthy of being called wine consistently coming out of Indian wineries. That is, only with the threat of imports forcing the Indian companies to act.

The moral of the story is that consumers need to force companies to act. Reward good winemaking; punish shoddy winemaking. Do support the Indian wineries, though. They are capable of making good quality wines, they only need the encouragement and incentive to do so.

As for me, I would rather drink any of the Indian wines listed in the BEST WINE BUYS (Appendix) any day than the sort of imports we usually get served. Between Gallo and IVY Shiraz, there is no question I would go for the IVY.

Indian wine has had a chequered past, but it has a glorious future. You can help the future to materialize.

Cheers!!

APPENDICES

APPENDIX I

INDIA'S BEST RED, WHITE, ROSÉ & SPARKLING WINE

PRODUCER	WINE	VARIETAL(S)
Indage	Ivy 2003	Shiraz
Blue Star	Bluefolds 2004	Sauvignon Blanc
Vinsura	Rosé 2004	Cabernet Sauvignon/ Local White
Sula	Brut 2003	Blend of Local Whites

THE BEST INDIAN WINE BUYS (VALUE FOR MONEY)

PRODUCER	WINE	VARIETAL(S)
Indage	Ivy 2003	Shiraz
Dajeebah	Merlot 2004	Merlot
Blue Star	Bluefolds 2004	Syrah
Flamingo	Zinfandel 2004	Zinfandel
Grover	Cabernet/Shiraz 2004	Cabernet/Shiraz
Flamingo	Cabernet/Shiraz 2004	Cabernet/Shiraz
Sula	Brut 2003	Blend
Blue Star	Bluefolds 2004	Sauvignon Blanc
Blue Star	Bluefolds 2004	Chenin Blanc
N.D.	Hoor 2003	Chenin / Sauvignon Blanc
Grover	Viognier 2004	Viognier/Clairette
Sula	Madera Rosé 2003	Local varieties
Vinsura	Rosé 2004	Cab-Sav/Local White

STYLE	EVALUATION	PRICE	PAGE
Red	Excellent	360	65
White	Very Good	330	44
Rosé	Good	360	93
Sparkling	Very Good	550	85

STYLE	EVALUATION	PRICE	PAGE
Red	Excellent	360	65
Red	Very Good	312	48
Red	Very Good	350	43
Red	Very Good	353	52
Red	Very Good	360	57
Red	Very Good	369	52
Sparkling	Very Good	550	85
White	Very Good	330	44
White	Very Good	330	43
White	Good	340	74
White	Good	360	58
Rosé	Good	205	89
Rosé	Good	360	93

THE BEST INDIAN WINES (OF EACH VARIETAL)

PRODUCER	WINE	VARIETAL(S)
Indage	Shiraz	Ivy 2003
Dajeebah	Merlot	Merlot 2004
Flamingo	Zinfandel	Zinfandel 2004
Flamingo	Cabernet/Shiraz	Cabernet/Shiraz 2004
Indage	Malbec	Ivy 2004
N.D.	Cabernet Sauvignon	Cabernet Sauvignon 200
Blue Star	Sauvignon Blanc	Bluefolds 2004
Vinsura	Chenin Blanc	Chenin Blanc 2003
Dajeebah	Chardonnay	Chardonnay 2004
Indage	Viognier	Ivy 2004

OTHER GOOD INDIAN WINES (ASCENDING PRICE)

PRODUCER	WINE	VARIETAL(S)
Sailo	Mark Antony 2004	Cab-Sav/Isabella
Saikripa	Cabernet/Merlot 2003	Cabernet/Merlot
Dajeebah	Syrah 2004	Syrah
Vinsura	Zinfandel 2004	Zinfandel
N.D.	Cabernet/Syrah 2003	Cabernet/Syrah
Flamingo	Chenin Blanc 2004	Chenin Blanc
Vinsura	Sauvignon Blanc 2004	Sauvignon Blanc
Greno	Chenin Blanc 2004	Chenin Blanc
Greno	Sauvignon Blanc 2004	Sauvignon Blanc
Indage	Marquis de Pompadour 2004	Blend

STYLE	EVALUATION	PRICE	PAGE
Red	Excellent	360	65
Red	Very Good	312	48
Red	Very Good	353	52
Red	Very Good	369	52
Red	Very Good	425	66
Red	Good	460	72
White	Very Good	330	44
White	Very Good	350	92
White	Good	402	49
White	Good	460	64

STYLE	EVALUATION	PRICE	PAGE
Red	Good	257	80
Red	Good	349	79
Red	Good	384	48
Red	Good	400	93
Red	Good	492	73
White	Good	326	51
White	Good	395	94
White	Good	396	53
White	Good	400	54
Sparkling	Good	600	63

APPENDIX II

Glossary and pronunciation Guide

ACID
Imparts a tangy or sour taste to wine, detectible especially on the back and sides of the tongue and mouth.

A.O.C.
Abbreviation for 'Appelation d'Origine Contrôlée,' the French classification system for wines (and other agricultural products). See the Classification Chart in the first section of Part Three.

AROMA
The smell of the grapes in a wine.

ASSEBLAGE
(A-sum-BLAHJ): The blending of wines to create a specifically desired result.

AUSLESE
(OUSE-lay-zeh): Sweet white German wine made from selected bunches of late-harvested grapes.

A.V.A.
Abbreviation for American Viticultural Area, the USA's version of AOC.

BEAUJOLAIS
(Bo-zho-LAY): A light fruity red wine from southern Burgundy in France.

BEERENAUSLESE
(Bear-en-OUSE-lay-ze): A full-bodied, sweet German white wine made from the rich sweet grapes affected by botrytis. See the Classification Chart in the first section of Part Three.

BLANC DE BLANCS
(Blahnk deh BLAHNK): White wine made from white grapes.

BLANC DE NOIR
(Blahnk deh NWAHR): White wine made from black (red) grapes.

BOTRYTIS (Bow-TRIED-iss)
Mould that grows onto grapes – also called 'noble rot' – that is necessary to make the rich, sweet wines of Sauternes in France as well as the German Beerenauslese and Trockenbeerenauslese.

BOTTLES
Each region in each wine-growing country uses specific bottles for specific styles of wine. Bottles are pretty universally sized in terms of capacity. A half-bottle is 37.5 cl, and a bottle is 75 cl. There are also 1 litre bottles, usually used for lower quality wines. There are also special larger sizes, usually reserved for very high quality wines and Champagnes (sparkling wines): 1.5 l (or 2 bottles) is called a Magnum, 4 bottles is a Jeroboam, Rehoboam is 6 bottles, Methusaleh is 8 bottles, Salmanazar is 12 bottles, Balthazar is 16 bottles, and the biggest is Nebuchadnezzar holding 20 bottles (15 liters)!

BOUQUET (Boo-KAY)
The smell of a wine.

BRUT (Brute)
The driest style of Champagne.

CABERNET SAUVIGNON (Cah-burr-NAY Sow-vee-NYOH)
The most important red-wine grape, often shortened to Cab-Sav.

CEPAGE (SAY-pahj)
The different grape varieties used in the blend of a wine.

CHAPTALIZATION
The addition of sugar to the must (freshly pressed grape juice) before fermentation.

CHARDONNAY (Shahr-dun-NAY)
The most important and expensive white grape, from which nearly all French Burgundy white wines are made.

CHATEAU (Shah-TOH)
In France, a house attached to a vineyard having a specific number of acres with winemaking and storage facilities on the property.

CHATEAUNEUF-DU-PAPE (Shah-toh-NUFF-dew-POP)
An excellent and affordable red wine from the southern Rhône valley in France.

CHENIN BLANC (Sha-nin BLAHNK)
A white grape grown primarily in the Loire valley in France, but also widely planted in California and India.

CHIANTI (Key-AHN-tee)
A basic red wine from the Tuscany region in Italy.

CORKED
A fault in a bottle of wine caused either by a bad (dirty, infected, impure) cork, or by air seeping into the bottle during storing or ageing.

COSECHA (Coh-SAY-cha)
The word for 'harvest' in Spanish.

CRIANZA (Cree-AHN-za)
The most basic and least expensive quality level of Rioja wine.

CUVE CLOSE (Q-VAY Cloz)
Process of making sparkling wines where, unlike in the Champagne method, the fermentation occurs in steel tanks.

DECANTING
Pouring wine into a carafe in order to separate the sediment from the wine.

DEMI-SEC (Deh-mee SECK)
Champagne or sparkling wine containing a high level of residual sugar.

D.O.C.
Abbreviation for 'Denominazione di Origine Controllata,' the classification system of Italy. See the Classification Chart in the first section of Part Three.

D.O.C.G.
The highest classification in Italy – the G means 'guaranteed.' See the Classification Chart in the first section of Part Three.

ENOLOGY (En-OL-o-gy)
The study of wine, also spelled 'Oenology.' Winemakers are usually enologists.

ESTATE-BOTTLED
Wine that is produced and bottled by the vineyard's owner.

EXTRA-DRY
Less dry than Brut (Champagne), but less sweet than demi-sec.

FILTRATION
The removal of deposits in a wine before bottling, used in modern winemaking.

FERMENTATION
With respect to wine, it is the process of grape juice turning into wine.

GAMAY (Gah-MAY)
A red grape used to make French Beaujolais.

GRENACHE (Gray-NASH)
Called Garnacha in Spain, this is a medium-sized, thin-skinned grape used in the Rhône Valley in France and in the Rioja in Spain. Its must can give wines of up to 16% alcohol, so Grenache is often blended with other wines to give body and alcohol.

HECTARE
A metric measure equal to 2.471 acres.

HECTOLITRE
A metric measure equal to 26.42 gallons.

HALBTROCKEN
German word for 'half-dry,' or semi-sweet.

KABINETT (Kah-bee-NETT)
Light, semi-dry German wine. See the Classification Chart in the first section of Part Three.

MALBEC
Excellent red wine grape, widely cultivated around Cahor in South-Central France. It gives a well-balanced wine of considerable finesse.

MALOLACTIC FERMENTATION
The 'malo' is a biochemical process that converts the hard malic

acid (found in apples) of unripe grapes into the soft lactic acid (found in milk), releasing a tiny amount of CO_2. This is vital for red wines, but optional for other styles.

MERLOT (Mer-LOW)
Famous red-wine grape considered second only to Cabernet Savignon.

METHODE CHAMPENOISE
(May-TUD Sham-pen-WAHZ)
Also called Methode traditionelle, it is the special 5-step method by which French Champagnes are made.

MICROCLIMATE
An area with a climate within a climate that affects the quality or characteristics of grapes grown in the area.

MOUSSEUX (Moo-SOW)
The word used in France for sparkling wines that are not made in Champagne.

MUSCADELLE
White wine grape of the Bordeaux country, where it is never used alone. It is often added at never more than 10% with other varieties in order to give Muscat (nutmeg) character.

MUST
Fresh grape juice from which wine is created by fermentation.

NEBBIOLO (Nay-bee-OW-low)
The outstanding red wine grape of Italy, at its best in Piedmonte.

NEGOCIANT (Na-go-see-YANT)
A merchant who buys, stores and sells wine.

NOSE
Term used to describe the bouquet and aroma of a wine.

PETILLANT (Pet-ee-YAHN)
A wine that very slightly sparkles, often as a result of very small-scale bottle fermentation.

PHYLLOXERA (Fill-LOCK-she-rah)
A grape louse or pest that eats away at vines and destroys them; American root stalks are resistant, and therefore most of the world's vineyards are planted with European vines grafted onto American root stalks.

PINOTAGE (PEE-noh-taj)
A cross between Pinot Noir and Cinsault (a Southern Rhône red grape) developed in 1925, used often in South Africa, producing rustic, high-tuned wines.

PINOT NOIR (PEE-noh NWAHR)
Classic red grape of Burgundy in France. It requires great attention because it is difficult to grow. The skins of the Pinot are thinner than that of Cab-Sav, and thus the wine tends to be more subtle but less tannic.

QUALITÄTSWEIN (Kval-ee-TATES-vine)
German word designating 'quality wine.' See the Classification Chart in the first section of Part Three.

QUALITÄTSWEIN MIT PRÄDIKAT (Kval-ee-TATES-vine mit pray-dee-KAHT)
The highest level of quality German wine under the German classification system. See the Classification Chart in the first section of Part Three.

RESERVA
Term designating that the wine has extra ageing – often seen on Italian, Spanish, Portuguese and Chilean wines. In the English-speaking world (found on Australian and on Indian wine labels), this is called 'Reserve.'

RESIDUAL SUGAR
The sugar remaining in the wine after the fermentation process is complete; it indicates how dry or sweet a wine is.

RIESLING
A noble and expensive white wine grape that flourishes in cool climates like Alsace in France, and Germany. Good Rieslings can also be found in California and Australia.

RIOJA (Ree-OH-ha)
A wine region in Spain.

SANGIOVESE (San-jee-ow-VAY-say)
Excellent red wine grape of Italy, thrives in Tuscany, more specifically, in Chianti.

SAUTERNES (Saw-TAIRN)
A sweet white wine from the Bordeaux region in France.

SAUVIGNON BLANC (SOH-veen-yown BLAHNK)

A white grape grown primarily in the Loire valley in France, and in Graves and Sauternes in Bordeaux. It currently makes some of the best white wines in India.

SEKT (zekt)

German sparkling wine.

SOMMELIER (So-mel-YAY)

French term for cellarmaster or wine steward.

SPÄTLESE (SHPATE-lay-zuh)

White German wine made from grapes picked later than the normal harvest. See the Classification Chart in the first section of Part III.

SPUMANTE (Spu-MANT-eh)

Italian sparkling wine (Prosecco, actually a grape name, is another term used for Italian sparkling wine).

STAINLESS-STEEL TANK

Container that can be kept clean and temperature controlled, used for fermentation in modern winemaking.

SULPHUR DIOXIDE

Chemical used in grape growing and winemaking as a sterilising agent, preservative and antioxidant.

TANNIN

A natural compound found on/in the skins, stems and pips (seeds) of grapes, and also in the wooden barrels used for aging wine. Tannins impart bitterness to wine, giving it structure and longevity.

TEMPRANILLO (Tem-pra-NIY-ow)

The Rioja grape par excellence, making up 50-80% or sometimes even 100% of the red wine from the Rioja. It is thick skinned and intensely black, and gives wine of good acidity.

TORRONTES (Tohr-ROHN-tayss)

A white grape variety from Galicia, Spain, gaining use especially in Argentina to make racy, highly aromatic wines.

TROCKEN (Troh-ken)

German word for 'dry.'

TROCKENBEERENAUSLESE
(Troh-ken-bear-en-OUSE-lay-zuh)

The richest, sweetest and costliest German wine made from

specially hand selected botrytis-affected grapes. See the Classification Chart in the first section of Part Three.

TUSCANY
A famous and beautiful wine region in Italy.

UGNI BLANC (Uhn-yee BLAHNK)
Called Trebbiano in Italy, is a grape variety that makes very light wines, and the juice is usually distilled—e.g., for making Cognac and Armagnac. The best wine can get with this grape is light, fresh, everyday drinking wine.

VARIETAL WINE
A wine labelled with the predominant grape variety used to make it rather than the region from which it derives.

VIN DE PAYS (Van deh Pay-EE)
Called VDP wine, it is part of the French classification or AOC system, standing one step below VDQS. VDP wines are often varietal wines of good value. See the Classification Chart in the first section of Part Three.

VINTAGE
The year grapes are harvested.

VIOGNIER (Vee-on-eey-AY)
An ancient white grape variety used in the Rhône region in France, tending to produce full-bodied, earthy wines, with good colour and rich bouquet.

VITIS VINIFERA (VEE-tiss Vih-NIFF-er-ah)
A European grape species used to make the best wines of the world.

VIURA
Also known as the Macabeo in other parts of Spain, the Viura is a prominent white wine grape for the Rioja whites.

ZINFANDEL
A red grape grown primarily in California, also now being tried out in India.

Lotus Collection

First published in 2006
The Lotus Collection
An imprint of Roli Books Pvt. Ltd.
M-75, G.K. II Market, New Delhi 110 048
Phones: ++91 (011) 2921 2271, 2921 2782
2921 0886, Fax: ++91 (011) 2921 7185
E-mail: roli@vsnl.com; Website:
rolibooks.com
Also at Varanasi, Bangalore, Jaipur, Bombay
and the Netherlands

Design: Arati Subramanyam
Layout: Kumar Raman

ISBN: 81-7436-434-X
Rs. 295

Printed and bound in Tan Prints (India) Pvt. Ltd